YORK NOTES

ANIMAL FARM

GEORGE ORWELL

NOTES BY WANDA OPALINSKA

PEARSON

YORK
PRESS

YORK PRESS
322 Old Brompton Road, London SW5 9JH

PEARSON EDUCATION LIMITED
Edinburgh Gate, Harlow,
Essex CM20 2JE, United Kingdom

Associated companies, branches and representatives throughout the world

First published 1997
New editions 2002 and 2011
This new and fully revised edition 2017

10 9 8 7

ISBN 978–1–4479–8213–5

Illustrated by John Rabon; and Moreno Chiacchiera (page 59 only)
Phototypeset by Carnegie Book Production
Printed in Great Britain by Ashford Colour Press Ltd

Photo credits: Skylines/Shutterstock for page 9 top / Sonia Alves-Polidori/Shutterstock for page 12 bottom / Kiwisoul/Shutterstock for page 13 middle / Eric Isselee/Shutterstock for page 14 bottom / Jeff Baumgart/Shutterstock for page 21 / Stephen Dukelow/Shutterstock for page 27 bottom / Peter Lorimer/Shutterstock page 29 bottom / Andrew Roland/Shutterstock for page 33 bottom / English School/Getty Images for page 35 bottom left/ Hulton Archive/Getty Images for page 35 bottom right/ VLADJ55/Shutterstock for page 36 bottom / PeJo/Shutterstock for page 37 bottom / Everett Collection Historical/Alamy for page 38 bottom / Topsy4/Alamy for page 39 bottom / Art_man/Shutterstock for page 40 bottom / corund/Shutterstock for page 41 bottom / 1000 Words/Shutterstock for page 42 bottom / Perutskyi Petro/Shutterstock for page 44 bottom / DragoNika/Shutterstock for page 45 bottom / anakondasp/Thinkstock for page 46 bottom / stockphoto mania/Shutterstock for page 47 middle / FPG Archive Photos/Getty Images for page 48 middle / mariocigic/Shutterstock for page 48 bottom / Luisma Tapia/Shutterstock for page 49 bottom / Tischenko Irina/Shutterstock for page 53 bottom / Hulton Archive/Getty Images for page 55 top / Roman Sigaev/Shutterstock for page 56 top / Olinchuk/Shutterstock for page 62 top / homydesign/Shutterstock for page 63 middle / Holy Kuchera/Shutterstock for page 64 top / Matt Gibson/Shutterstock for page 66 middle / wavebreakmedia/Shutterstock for page 75 middle

CONTENTS

PREPARING FOR ASSESSMENT

HOW WILL I BE ASSESSED ON MY WORK ON *ANIMAL FARM*?

All exam boards are different but whichever course you are following, your work will be examined through these four Assessment Objectives:

Assessment Objectives	Wording	Worth thinking about ...
AO1	Read, understand and respond to texts. Students should be able to: • maintain a critical style and develop an informed personal response • use textual references, including quotations, to support and illustrate interpretations.	• How well do I know what happens, what characters say, do, etc.? • What do *I* think about the key ideas in the text? • How can I support my viewpoint in a really convincing way? • What are the best quotations to use and when should I use them?
AO2	Analyse the language, form and structure used by a writer to create meanings and effects, using relevant subject terminology where appropriate.	• What specific things does the writer 'do'? What choices has Orwell made? (Why this particular word, phrase or paragraph here? Why does this event happen at this point?) • What effects do these choices create – irony? Humour? Pity?
AO3	Show understanding of the relationships between texts and the contexts in which they were written.	• What can I learn about society from the text? (What does it tell me about politics and power, for example?) • What was happening in the world in Orwell's time? Can I see it reflected in the text?
AO4	Use a range of vocabulary and sentence structures for clarity, purpose and effect, with accurate spelling and punctuation.	• How accurately and clearly do I write? • Are there small errors of grammar, spelling and punctuation I can get rid of?

Look out for the Assessment Objective labels throughout your York Notes Study Guide – these will help to focus your study and revision!

The text used in these Notes is the Heinemann New Windmill edition, 1994.

HOW TO USE YOUR YORK NOTES STUDY GUIDE

You are probably wondering what is the best and most efficient way to use your York Notes Study Guide on *Animal Farm*. Here are three possibilities:

A **step-by-step** study and revision guide	A **'dip-in' support** when you need it	A **revision guide** after you have finished the text
Step 1: Read Part Two as you read the text, as a companion to help you study it. **Step 2:** When you need to, turn to Parts Three to Five to focus your learning. **Step 3:** Then, when you have finished, use Parts Six and Seven to hone your exam skills, revise and practise for the exam.	Perhaps you know the text quite well, but you want to check your understanding and practise your exam skills? Just look for the section you think you need most help with and go for it!	You might want to use the Notes after you have finished your study, using Parts Two to Five to check over what you have learned, and then work through Parts Six and Seven in the immediate weeks leading up to your exam.

HOW WILL THE GUIDE HELP YOU STUDY AND REVISE?

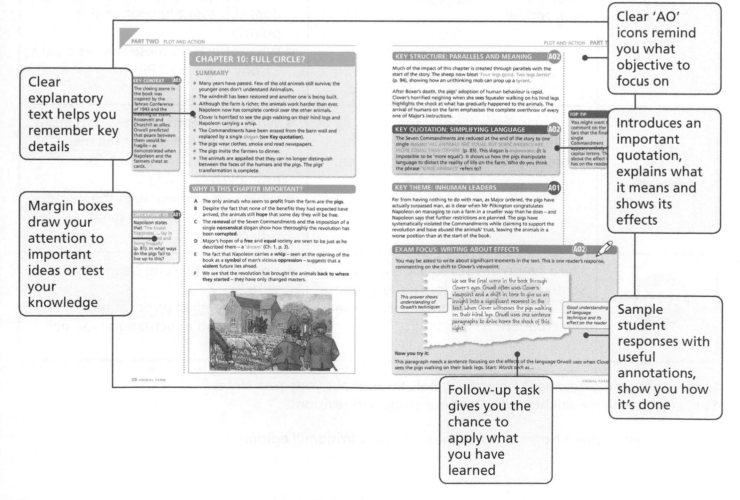

Clear explanatory text helps you remember key details

Margin boxes draw your attention to important ideas or test your knowledge

Clear 'AO' icons remind you what objective to focus on

Introduces an important quotation, explains what it means and shows its effects

Sample student responses with useful annotations, show you how it's done

Follow-up task gives you the chance to apply what you have learned

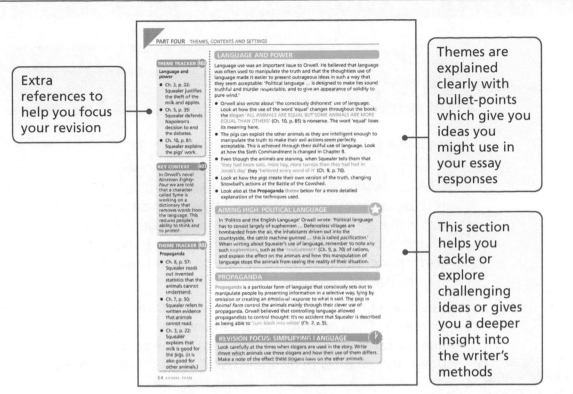

Extra references to help you focus your revision

Themes are explained clearly with bullet-points which give you ideas you might use in your essay responses

This section helps you tackle or explore challenging ideas or gives you a deeper insight into the writer's methods

Parts Two to Five end with a **Progress and revision check**:

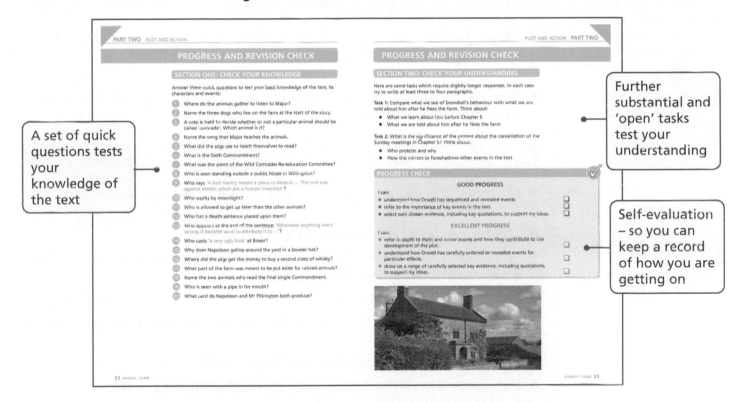

A set of quick questions tests your knowledge of the text

Further substantial and 'open' tasks test your understanding

Self-evaluation – so you can keep a record of how you are getting on

Don't forget Parts Six and Seven, with advice and practice on **improving your writing skills**:

- Focus on **difficult areas** such as **'context'** and **'inferences'**
- **Short snippets** of **other students' work** to show you how it's done (or not done!)
- Three annotated **sample responses** to a task **at different levels**, with **expert comments**, to help you judge your own level
- **Practice questions**
- **Answers** to the **Progress and revision checks** and **Checkpoint** margin boxes

Now it's up to you! Don't forget – there's even more help on our website with more sample answers, essay planners and even online tutorials. Go to www.yorknotes.com to find out more.

PLOT SUMMARY: WHAT HAPPENS IN *ANIMAL FARM*?

REVISION FOCUS: MAKE SURE YOU KNOW THE KEY EVENTS

It is important that you know all the key events in the story so that you can write about them confidently in the exam. *Animal Farm* is an allegory, so it is vital that you identify which moments in the story correspond with a historical event to show how Orwell uses this to get his political point across to his readers.

Read **An allegory of Russian history** and **Direct parallels** in **Part Four: Contexts**. Then go through the summaries below, highlighting each allegorical event. Find each moment in the text and reread it. Write down the political point that Orwell makes with each event.

TOP TIP (A01)

Make a note of the times when the animals are on the verge of protesting about events on the farm. Think about what stops them on each occasion.

CHAPTER 1: MAJOR'S VISION

- Major the boar, the most 'highly regarded' (Ch. 1, p. 1) animal on Manor Farm, tells the other animals about a dream he has had, in which animals live free from slavery and exploitation.
- Major's speech inspires the animals to rebel against mankind and create their own society, based on Major's ideas of equality and freedom.

CHAPTERS 2 AND 3: REVOLUTION

- Mr Jones, the farmer, is driven out of the farm. Mrs Jones flees too, followed by the raven Moses.
- The farm is renamed Animal Farm.
- The Seven Commandments are written on the barn wall by Snowball as a permanent reminder of the new farm rules.
- The animals discover that the pigs have taken the milk and apples.
- The animals work hard to get the harvest in and do a better job than Mr Jones ever did.
- Snowball teaches the animals to read and write.
- Napoleon takes the puppies away to be educated in private.
- Squealer tells the animals that the pigs have taken the milk and apples for everyone's benefit.

CHAPTERS 4 AND 5: NAPOLEON SEIZES POWER

- The animals try to spread the revolutionary ideas of Animal Farm across the countryside.
- Two neighbouring farmers, Mr Frederick and Mr Pilkington, are frightened that the revolution will spread to their own farms. They help Mr Jones to attack Animal Farm.

- Snowball leads the animals to victory in the Battle of the Cowshed.
- Mollie vanishes from the farm.
- The conflict between Napoleon and Snowball increases.
- After he disagrees with Napoleon about the building of the windmill, Snowball is attacked by Napoleon's dogs and driven from the farm.
- Napoleon tells the other animals that there will be no more debates – the pigs will make the decisions.

CHAPTERS 6 AND 7: WORKING LIKE SLAVES

- The animals work harder than ever before.
- The windmill runs into difficulties.
- Napoleon decides to trade with humans.
- The pigs move into Mr Jones's house and sleep in beds.
- The animals face starvation. Napoleon takes Mr Whymper, his solicitor, around the farm and tricks him into thinking that the gossip about the famine is untrue.
- Napoleon holds a terrifying 'show trial', accusing his opponents of ludicrous crimes. The accused animals are publicly executed. The other animals are frightened and confused.

CHAPTERS 8 AND 9: BOXER IS BETRAYED

- The pigs continue to alter the Commandments on the wall to justify their actions.
- The animals work harder than they did under Mr Jones but eat far less.
- Napoleon's trade with Mr Frederick causes problems and the humans destroy the finished windmill.
- The new young pigs are to be educated separately.
- Moses returns to the farm.
- Boxer collapses in the quarry. The pigs sell Boxer to the owner of the knacker's yard as he is too weak to work. They use the money they get from selling him to buy more whisky.

CHAPTER 10: FULL CIRCLE?

- The farm is richer than ever but the animals also work harder than ever.
- Clover sees the pigs walking on their hind legs and Napoleon carrying a whip.
- The Commandments have been erased and replaced by a single slogan: 'ALL ANIMALS ARE EQUAL BUT SOME ANIMALS ARE MORE EQUAL THAN OTHERS' (Ch. 10, p. 85).
- The pigs invite the farmers to dinner.
- The animals look in through the farmhouse window and can no longer see the difference between the pigs and the humans.

CHECKPOINT 1 (A02)

Why are the Seven Commandments so important in the book?

CHAPTER 1: MAJOR'S VISION

SUMMARY

- Mr Jones, the owner of Manor Farm, tries to lock the farm up for the night but is too drunk to do it properly. He then goes to bed.
- Major, the 'Middle White boar' (p. 1), the most respected animal on the farm, calls everyone to the barn for a meeting.
- Major tells the animals about his dream: a future in which the animals can live on the farm in peace and freedom, without being exploited by humans.
- Major gives the animals a set of rules for them to live by to avoid becoming like their enemy, man.
- Major's dream unites the animals. They excitedly sing 'Beasts of England' (p. 7), waking Mr Jones.
- Mr Jones fires his gun and frightens the animals, who return to their beds.

WHY IS THIS CHAPTER IMPORTANT?

A It introduces the **setting** (a farm), **Mr Jones** and the **animals** to the reader.

B Major's speech establishes an **idealised vision** of the **future** in contrast to the animals' **present suffering** under Mr Jones – and their later suffering under the pigs.

C Orwell encourages us to feel **sympathetic** towards some of the animals to heighten the pathos of their treatment by the pigs later in the story.

D Major's **revolutionary** vision **predicts** many events that later come true – such as Boxer's eventual fate. The irony is that this occurs under the pigs' tyranny, not man's.

KEY CONTEXT: MAJOR AND MARX

Major's speech draws from the work of the German philosopher Karl Marx – and in particular the *Communist Manifesto* (1848), which Marx co-wrote with Friedrich Engels. Lenin, the first Soviet leader, based many of his ideas on Marx's thinking. Major claims that the life of a farm animal is one of 'misery and slavery' (p. 3) because the animals are exploited by man – their only real enemy – who 'consumes without producing' (p. 4) and doesn't reward them for what he takes.

Marx believed that capitalists behave in the same way that Major thinks humans do, by exploiting the workers or proletariat, who never see the rewards of their labour. Marx thought that this would only stop if the proletariat revolted against the capitalists.

Orwell makes us sympathetic to this Marxist argument by listing the various ways in which man makes the animals suffer. The only solution is to rebel against man.

CHECKPOINT 2 **A02**

How are the animals' names appropriate to their roles in the story? Give at least one example.

KEY THEME: EQUALITY

Major suggests that the animals can create a new, equal society, as 'All animals are equal' (p. 6). In Chapter 2, Snowball, Napoleon and Squealer develop these ideas into 'a complete system of thought' (p. 9) called Animalism. Although Orwell uses Major to emphasise the need for 'perfect unity' (p. 5) and equality in Chapter 1, there are signs that this is harder to achieve than the animals first think. Directly after Major's speech, the dogs attack the rats, which appears to contradict what Major has just said. Orwell seems to suggest that human behaviour makes political systems vulnerable to failure.

AIMING HIGH: HOW ORWELL ESTABLISHES HIS CHARACTERS

When writing about the characters, you should show how the descriptions in this chapter prepare us for how the animals react to events later on – don't just list what they do without explaining *why* it is significant. You should also mention the language Orwell uses to describe them. What effect does this have on us as readers?

For example, Boxer and Clover are shown 'walking very slowly and setting down their vast hairy hoofs with great care lest there should be some small animal concealed in the straw' (p. 2), so it doesn't surprise us that they both behave compassionately later in the book. The word 'small' emphasises both the carthorses' size and power and their concern for those weaker and more vulnerable than themselves. Clover recalls this incident later in Chapter 7 – in very different circumstances. How does this incident appear then?

CHECKPOINT 3 A01

Are there any other ways in which Orwell makes us feel sympathetic towards the animals in Chapter 1?

TOP TIP (A02)

Look at how the language used by the pigs differs from that of the other animals in the book. What effect does this create? What is Orwell's message here?

KEY QUOTATION: MAJOR'S RULES (A01)

'No animal must ever live in a house, or sleep in a bed, or wear clothes, or drink alcohol, or smoke tobacco, or touch money or engage in trade. All the habits of Man are evil. And, above all, no animal must ever tyrannize over his own kind. ... No animal must ever kill any other animal. All animals are equal.' (p. 6)

This extract from Major's speech forms the basis of the Seven Commandments that the pigs create in the next chapter. This passage also acts as the moral core of the book. When writing about this speech, look at Major's use of imperatives: 'No animal must ever...'. These are unambiguous instructions to the animals. (Do you think they act as orders – and if so, what does this tell us about the pigs?)

EXAM FOCUS: WRITING ABOUT EQUALITY (A02)

You may be asked to write about how equal the animals are at the beginning of *Animal Farm*. Read this example by one student, commenting on this issue:

Precise point, well made

Orwell's animals aren't as equal as they at first appear in the story's opening: the pigs make their way to the front of the meeting, as though this prime position is naturally theirs. The cat looks for the warmest place to sit - and doesn't listen to a word that is said.

This response shows a good understanding of the significance of the seating in the barn, which could be developed further

A good grasp of character and significance but could be developed to consider the way in which this might undermine Major's message of equality

Now you try it:

This paragraph needs a final sentence to explain what Orwell is suggesting here about some of the difficulties the animals will face when making Major's utopia a reality. Start with: *Orwell seems to suggest that ...*

CHAPTER 2: REVOLUTION

SUMMARY

- Snowball, Napoleon and Squealer turn Major's ideas into 'a complete system of thought' (p. 9) called Animalism.

- The pigs hold secret meetings to spread Animalism to the others but encounter some obstacles.

- Mr Jones and his men forget to feed the animals, who rebel against him and drive the humans off the farm. The animals then enter the farmhouse and destroy the whips and other symbols of tyranny.

- Napoleon and Snowball (two young, literate boars) take charge, using Major's instructions to plan the Revolution and create a free and equal society.

- Manor Farm is renamed Animal Farm. Orwell tells us it is a more efficient and happier place than before. The animals seem to have created a perfect society.

- The pigs paint the Seven Commandments on the wall for all to read but, despite Snowball's literacy classes, few of the other animals can read.

- The pigs milk the cows. While the animals are at the harvest, unknown to them, Napoleon sees that the milk is 'attended to' (p. 16). When they get back, they find that the milk has vanished.

WHY IS THIS CHAPTER IMPORTANT?

A   We see that the **pigs** are 'generally recognized as being the **cleverest** of the animals' (p. 9). They seem to be **'natural' leaders**.

B   Not everyone supports Major's revolutionary ideals. Some animals react with 'stupidity and apathy' (p. 9), some still feel loyal to Mr Jones and others believe Moses's stories of **Sugarcandy Mountain**. These differences in opinion will bring problems later on. (Notice that the animals also don't expect the Revolution to happen soon – it is a 'sudden uprising' (pp. 11–12)).

C   Mr Jones's idle, self-indulgent behaviour and his **neglect** of the farm is set up in detail by Orwell so that we think Jones's expulsion from the farm is a good thing. Orwell makes it clear that the animals' **rebellion** is **justified**.

D   This chapter shows the effect of Major's ideas on the animals – it gives them 'a completely new outlook on life' (p. 9). We think that the animals' new society will be **equal** and democratic. Orwell drives this home to us by renaming the farm – a **symbol** of this fresh start.

CHECKPOINT 4   (A02)

Look at the descriptions of Napoleon and Snowball. How do these prepare you for what happens later in the book?

KEY CONTEXT   (A03)

For Orwell, the disappearance of the cows' milk was the turning point of the book. Orwell wrote in a letter to a friend: 'If the other animals had had the sense to put their foot down then, it would have been all right.'

TOP TIP   (A01)

You might want to comment on the fact that the farm is called Manor Farm. This reminds us of the feudal system, suggesting that Jones is clinging to the past and cannot adapt to change.

AIMING HIGH: ORWELL'S FORESHADOWING OF LATER EVENTS

To demonstrate your understanding of the book, show how Orwell presents the difficulties the pigs face in convincing the other animals of their ideas to foreshadow events later in the story.

While Mollie only thinks in terms of how a rebellion might benefit her, even these benefits are signs of her enslavement to Mr Jones – she can't picture what freedom would be like or what real advantages it might hold. Orwell tells us twice about the 'stupidity' of the animals' reactions; some arguments are seen as 'elementary' (Ch. 2, p. 9). While apathy is also a problem, Orwell draws a clear intellectual divide between the pigs and other animals on the farm: even Boxer and Clover, the pigs' 'most faithful disciples' (Ch. 2, p. 10), aren't able to think for themselves.

The animals' inability to grasp the pigs' ideas – and their subsequent dependence on them – contributes to the problems they face later on. Even before the rebellion, we can see their gullibility being exploited by Moses.

KEY CONTEXT (A03)

In the Old Testament, Moses was the Hebrew prophet who led the Israelites out of Egypt to the Promised Land and gave them God's Ten Commandments. Why do you think Orwell chose this name for the deceitful raven?

KEY LANGUAGE: A NEW SOCIETY (A02)

Orwell leaves us in no doubt that the rebellion is a good thing. The description of the farm the morning after Mr Jones's expulsion is unusually poetic ('the clear morning light') and contains an evocative physical description of the animals' activities: they 'rolled in the dew', 'cropped mouthfuls of sweet summer grass', 'kicked up clods of the black earth and snuffed its rich scent' (p. 13). This more poetic language contrasts with the plain language in which the majority of the book is written, emphasising the significance of this moment.

The new dawn is symbolic as well as literal. It is as though the animals have woken from a sleep. We see them excitedly savour the fact that the farm now belongs to them. Orwell makes us aware of the scale of the animals' achievement: 'with speechless admiration ... they could hardly believe that it was all their own' (p. 13).

Orwell's description of the harvest shows how hard the animals have to work in their new lives but also that their unity and co-operation make the work much more successful.

CHECKPOINT 5 (A01)

The animals are said to be speechless in the other parts of the book too. Why is this a cause for concern?

TOP TIP: WRITING ABOUT THE REVOLUTION (A01)

Although Orwell leaves us in no doubt that the rebellion is a good thing for the farm as a whole, when writing about this chapter you need to show that not all of the animals feel the same way about life without Mr Jones. Moses flees the farm with Mrs Jones, while Mollie is concerned that the luxuries she enjoyed under Jones (such as sugar and ribbons) have gone too. More impressive responses will also notice Mollie's reaction to the farmhouse compared to that of the other animals: her self-interest and fascination with Mrs Jones's blue ribbon prevent her from understanding what the farmhouse symbolises to the other animals.

KEY SETTING: THE FARMHOUSE (A02)

The animal's reactions to the farmhouse are comic as well as touching. Their reluctance to enter it, and their reaction to it – they gaze at the 'unbelievable luxury' (p. 13) – emphasise the gulf between their lives and that of Mr Jones. The house is seen from the animals' perspective: to us, the burial of the hams is comic; to the animals, it is entirely proper.

At this stage all the animals are involved in making decisions on the farm – they all vote to keep the farmhouse as a museum. Their view of the luxuries inside will resonate later when Napoleon seizes the farmhouse for his own use.

TOP TIP (A01)

How would the revolution have been different if the other animals were able to read and write as well as the pigs? Go through the book and find points where you think the animals might have had a chance to question the pigs' actions. What prevents them from doing this?

TOP TIP: WRITING ABOUT THE SEVEN COMMANDMENTS (A02)

When the Seven Commandments are written on the barn wall, Snowball tells the animals that they form 'an unalterable law' (p. 15) for life on the farm. The Commandments are the foundations for the post-revolutionary society. You need to show that Orwell deliberately echoes Christianity's Ten Commandments here: the pigs' rules provide a quasi-religious code by which the animals will live (even though most of the animals cannot read …). You should also show how Orwell uses the Commandments structurally in the book to provide a framework by which we judge the pigs' later actions and chart the farm's gradual descent into tyranny.

KEY LANGUAGE: 'COMRADE' (A02)

The fact that the animals address each other as 'Comrade' is significant and helps to cement the allegorical nature of the story. While the word had previously been used as a way of addressing colleagues or co-workers, by the time Orwell was writing *Animal Farm* in the early 1940s 'comrade' had become strongly associated with Soviet Russia. The book's first readers would have had no doubt about which government was being depicted.

CHAPTER 3: UTOPIA?

SUMMARY

- The harvest is completed in record time, as the animals work hard under the supervision of the pigs.
- The animals are taught to read and write by Snowball.
- Napoleon takes the puppies away to raise them himself.
- Squealer tells the animals that the pigs have taken the apples and milk for everyone's benefit.

WHY IS THIS CHAPTER IMPORTANT?

A The **tone** at the start of this chapter creates a sense of **liberation** and continues the euphoric mood of Chapter 2. The description of the **harvest** echoes the rhetoric of **Major's speech**.

B It shows that the animals' behaviour after the rebellion is generally unselfish and as a result they are more successful than before. They are also rid of 'worthless parasitical' humans (p. 17).

C It sets out several ideas regarding **leadership** and **power**: Jones's rule was not, as some of the animals thought, simply a fact of life. The animals can do the job just as well – just not in the same way. Working together, the animals succeed far better than Jones ever did – a statement by Orwell on the power of democracy and **unity**. The idea of 'natural' leadership (p. 16) is also questioned: look at how the pigs rapidly gain power because of their **intelligence**.

D Orwell emphasises how crucial Boxer is to the new farm's success. He is 'the admiration of everybody' and 'the entire work of the farm seemed to rest upon his mighty shoulders' (p. 17). His **determination** is contrasted with the behaviour of Mollie and the cat, who can be described as **parasites**.

E We see that Snowball is an **innovator**: he organises various committees in an effort to help the animals. However, most of them are failures.

F There is **conflict** between Snowball and Napoleon.

KEY THEME: UNITY AND CONFLICT

Orwell emphasises the animals' unity. The phrase 'everyone worked according to his capacity' (p. 18) echoes a core socialist belief popularised by Marx: 'From each according to his ability, to each according to his need'. Orwell makes it clear to us that this equal utopian society is a socialist one: each individual works their hardest for the group: 'Nobody stole, nobody grumbled over his rations, the quarrelling and biting and jealousy ... had almost disappeared.' (p. 18). However, this quotation from the text also hints at some conflict, especially in the relationship between Napoleon and Snowball, which begins to disrupt life on the farm. Napoleon concentrates on building up his own power. We are given hints about how this is done but don't find out its full extent until later in the story.

CHECKPOINT 6 **A01**

What does each animal's reading ability tell you about them?

CHECKPOINT 7 **A02**

'Nobody stole, nobody grumbled over his rations, the quarrelling and biting and jealousy ... had almost disappeared' (p. 18). Why is the use of the word 'almost' significant here?

TOP TIP **A01**

This chapter satirises the way in which a crucial skill like reading can be misused. Make a list that includes each character and their attitude to reading. This will be useful to you when you chart what happens later in the book. How far do you think this lack of ability or interest on the animals' part is a factor in their exploitation?

KEY CHARACTERS: CLEVER PIGS? (A02)

The pigs are shown to be more intelligent than the other animals: 'With their superior knowledge it was natural that they should assume the leadership' (p. 16). By becoming the farm's managers, the pigs avoid physical work. At this point in the book this is not seen as sinister. We do, however, see that the pigs' intelligence is sometimes flawed: Snowball's committees have no real function as the animals don't really understand what Snowball tells them – this works against him in the end.

We also see how persuasive Squealer is when he defends the pigs' actions in a brilliant piece of rhetoric which is reinforced by his repeated threat of Mr Jones's return: 'Do you know what would happen if we pigs failed in our duty? Jones would come back!' (p. 22). Later, Squealer systematically distorts Major's Commandments, reflecting the gradual erosion of the animals' revolutionary ideals. The pigs' cleverness becomes a double-edged sword: although it means Animal Farm can survive, it also enables the pigs to exploit the other animals, for example, taking advantage of Boxer's gentleness to manipulate him later on.

KEY THEME: THE IMPORTANCE OF EDUCATION (A01)

Snowball's most important task is to teach the animals to read. Although we are told that his classes are 'a great success' and 'almost every animal on the farm was literate in some degree' (p. 20) the animals fail to make the most of the skills they have been taught. Muriel reads material from the rubbish dump, Benjamin says there is 'nothing worth reading' (p. 20) and Mollie simply indulges her own vanity. Boxer and Clover want to learn but don't have the ability to get beyond the basics. Snowball's attempts to encourage the animals to participate more in the revolution prove futile.

TOP TIP (A01)

Go through the chapter again, making a note of each time a reference is made to the cleverness of the pigs. Why does Orwell emphasise this so much?

CHECKPOINT 8 (A02)

Why does Squealer use the word 'duty' (p. 22) when defending the pigs' actions?

CHECKPOINT 9 (A02)

Look at the use of the word 'order' on page 22 of the text. What is starting to happen on the farm?

EXAM FOCUS: WRITING ABOUT EFFECTS (A02)

You may be asked to write about the effect of Orwell's use of language in the text. This is one reader's response, commenting on the description of the harvest:

| Some awareness of the effect of the writer's style |

> Orwell's style changes in Chapter 3. Unlike his usually plain, simple sentences, longer, more flowing sentences are used to create a sense of freedom. Orwell wants us to see the harvest as a highpoint: he repeats the word 'nobody' ('Nobody stole, nobody grumbled'), which emphasises the animals' unity.

| Good understanding of Orwell's choice of language and its effects |

Now you try it:

This paragraph needs a sentence to explain why Orwell shifts from discussing the animals in collective terms to focusing on two individual characters and how this undermines the unity of the harvest. Start: *The phrase 'almost nobody' tell us that …*

CHAPTER 4: THE BATTLE OF THE COWSHED

SUMMARY

- News of the rebellion spreads. The animals try to promote the revolutionary ideas of Animal Farm across the countryside.
- The farmers of the two neighbouring farms, Mr Frederick and Mr Pilkington, take steps to prevent an animal uprising.
- Mr Jones attempts to recapture Animal Farm with the help of men from Pinchfield and Foxwood farms.
- Snowball's brilliant tactics lead the animals to victory in what the animals decide to call the Battle of the Cowshed.

CHECKPOINT 10 **A01**

Why are all the humans in the book so unpleasant? How does this serve Orwell's purpose in writing *Animal Farm*?

WHY IS THIS CHAPTER IMPORTANT?

A   Orwell reminds us of what the animals are **revolting** against when he **introduces** the **humans**. We also see how **fragile** the new society is, and **vulnerable** to **attack from outside**.

B   The farmers **suppress** any signs of rebellion on neighbouring farms. Orwell again reminds us of humans' **oppressive**, selfish nature and introduces us to the farm's violent neighbours.

C   We are given another reminder of what is achieved when the animals are united: 'Even the cat' (p. 26) fights to protect the farm.

C   Snowball is seen as a brilliant **strategist**.

D   Boxer and Snowball both risk their lives to defend the farm and are praised as heroes of the battle. However, we see that – unlike Snowball – Boxer is **compassionate**, as Orwell emphasises when the carthorse is upset at injuring the stable-lad during the battle.

E   There are further signs that a **hierarchy** is developing: Napoleon and Snowball direct events and some animals are favoured.

KEY CHARACTER: SNOWBALL – A GREAT LEADER? (A01)

Like his allegorical counter-part, Trotsky, Snowball is seen as a capable leader. He anticipates the humans' attack and devises a carefully planned campaign in which the invaders are ambushed. Look carefully at Snowball's actions here – Napoleon later distorts these events to turn the animals against Snowball and improve his own reputation. However, we also notice Snowball's ruthless dismissal of human suffering: 'The only good human being is a dead one' (p. 26).

TOP TIP (A01)

Look carefully at the role each animal takes in the battle. Are any significant characters missing?

AIMING HIGH: *ANIMAL FARM* AS ALLEGORY ⭐

Animal Farm is commonly read as a political allegory. You should show in your writing how Orwell draws parallels between events in Russian history and those on Animal Farm. Lenin's revolution was threatened by invading forces in the same way as the farm is threatened in this chapter – and it was Trotsky's strategy that was central to the Bolshevik's victory. You should always link such parallels back to what Orwell was trying to achieve: what view do you think he expects us to have of the revolution's attempts to defend itself?

KEY CHARACTERS: PORTRAYAL OF THE HUMANS (A01)

All the humans in the book are portrayed as unpleasant. The farmers try to take advantage of Mr Jones's situation, while Mr Jones himself is a brute. The humans' cruelty reinforces Major's negative view of humanity. Orwell wants us to see that the revolution was necessary.

EXAM FOCUS: AN EMERGING HIERARCHY? (A01) ✏️

You might be asked to write about how Orwell presents the rising inequality of Animal Farm. Read this response by one student, commenting on the pigs' new-found love of military honours:

Shows a good grasp of the medals' symbolic significance

Slightly repetitive but the distinction between the main characters and the dead sheep is a sound one

The medals the animals receive – 'Animal Hero, First Class' and 'Animal Hero, Second Class' – show that already some animals are considered to be better than others. While we feel that Boxer and Snowball have deserved these rewards for their heroism, the distinction between their bravery and that of the dead sheep suggests that the animals are already creating a hierarchy among themselves: the dead sheep isn't even named.

Good comment on how Orwell presents the sheep – this could be expanded further by looking at the effects of Orwell's collective use of animals such as the dogs and the sheep

Now you try it:

This paragraph needs a sentence to explain how our view of the medals changes when Napoleon starts awarding them to himself. Start: *Later in the book …*

CHAPTER 5: NAPOLEON SEIZES POWER

SUMMARY

- Mollie vanishes and is rumoured to be happy serving under Mr Pilkington.
- The conflict between Napoleon and Snowball increases as their disagreements become more serious.
- Snowball suggests building a windmill, which brings the farm's divisions out into the open.
- Napoleon's dogs attack Snowball and he is forced to flee for his life.
- Once he has seized power, Napoleon abolishes the Sunday debates.
- Squealer tells the animals that the windmill will be built after all and that it was Napoleon's idea all along.

WHY IS THIS CHAPTER IMPORTANT?

A The **pigs** now **control** what happens on the farm; they **decide** 'all questions of farm policy' (p. 29).

B Plans for the windmill are simplified into slogans rather than discussed in reasoned speeches. Orwell argued elsewhere that **simplifying language** coarsens thought.

C On the allegorical level, the differing views of socialism held by Trotsky and Stalin are highlighted (see **Part Four: Themes**).

D Napoleon shows his contempt for **free speech**.

E Napoleon uses **violence** to establish **absolute control** over the animals. His coup has been planned for a long time. An immediate **parallel** is drawn between Napoleon and Mr Jones when we are told the dogs wagged their tails to Napoleon 'in the same way as the other dogs had been used to do to Mr Jones' (p. 34).

F The Sunday Meeting, instead of being a time when the animals agree their workload, becomes the assembly at which their **orders** are given.

G The chapter ends on a much **bleaker** note than that on which it opened.

KEY CHARACTER: NAPOLEON

Napoleon makes little response to Snowball's speeches, and when he does speak it is only to criticise Snowball. Napoleon's campaign against Snowball is carefully planned, as is demonstrated by his use of the sheep and dogs.

Snowball's exile and Napoleon's use of terror remove all opposition to the latter's plans. After Snowball's expulsion, any hope of a more just, equal life becomes unlikely. The farm is on its way to becoming a totalitarian society.

CHECKPOINT 11 A01

What does Mollie's love of sugar suggest?

TOP TIP A02

Make sure you explain why Napoleon's use of violence and intimidation marks a turning point in the story. Link this back to Major's speech.

CHECKPOINT 12 A01

What hints are there in this chapter that Napoleon has carefully planned the way in which he gains power?

KEY THEME: HOW DEMOCRACY IS UNDERMINED **A01**

Although the revolution is supposed to have created an equal society, in this chapter we see the animals slowly lose control over their lives. All decisions are taken by the pigs, although at first they claim that decisions are to be agreed by a majority vote. The animals' fickle nature (for example, changing their mind according to whoever is speaking) and their lack of intelligence make it easy for Napoleon to manipulate them.

The sheep, with their mindless bleating, effectively silence opposing opinions – no one else can be heard. The animals are uneasy about Napoleon's actions but cannot express what they feel.

CHECKPOINT 13 **A02**

In Chapter 5, how does Squealer persuade the animals to doubt their own opinions?

EXAM FOCUS: PROPAGANDA IN *ANIMAL FARM* **A02**

You could be asked to examine how Orwell presents the theme of propaganda in *Animal Farm*. This is how one reader tackled the subject:

> Squealer's propaganda is crucial to Napoleon's rise to power. Squealer's flattering description of Napoleon as a hero – his references to the leader's 'deep and heavy responsibility' and his 'sacrifice' – emphasises the gulf between the animals and their leader. By his skilful use of omissions and half-truths, not to mention outright lies and questionable evidence, Squealer succeeds in convincing the animals of Napoleon's fitness for power and justifies his actions.

Good, articulate opening, which is then well supported with textual references

Shows understanding of some of the techniques Squealer uses to manipulate the animals

Now you try it:

This paragraph needs a sentence to explain how the animals' lack of understanding makes Squealer's job easier. Start: *Squealer's job is made easier as …*

CHAPTER 6: WORKING LIKE SLAVES

SUMMARY

- The animals continue their hard labour, working a sixty-hour week and Sunday afternoons as well.
- The building of the windmill runs into difficulties.
- The harvest is poorer than the previous year.
- Napoleon tells the animals that he has decided to trade with the neighbouring farmers.
- The pigs move into the farmhouse and a Commandment is broken – the animals now sleep in beds. This is explained away by Squealer as necessary for the defence of the farm. An alteration to this Commandment is painted onto the wall.
- A violent storm destroys the windmill but Napoleon declares that it was sabotaged by Snowball and passes the death sentence upon him.
- Life for the animals continues to be hard as they try to rebuild the windmill. They are now fed at the same level as they were under Mr Jones. Things are going back to how they were.

KEY CONTEXT (A03)

The building of the windmill represents the rapid industrialisation of the Soviet Union. Stalin created Five-Year Plans which brought great hardship to the Russian people. What point is Orwell making here?

WHY IS THIS CHAPTER IMPORTANT?

A   The pigs use – or rather **misuse** – **language** to make the **sufferings** that they inflict upon the other animals sound **acceptable**. The **Commandments** are subtly **altered** to accommodate the pigs' behaviour, ideas are reduced to slogans and we see Squealer **manipulate** the animals with propaganda.

B   Napoleon's announcement about trading with other farms is a formality, as plans have already been made. We see him use **fear** and **intimidation** to suppress any protest.

C   The animals' hard work brings **suffering**. Their lives seem to be almost the same as under Jones.

D   Orwell contrasts the **hardship** suffered by the animals with the **luxurious** lifestyle enjoyed by the pigs to point up their **corruption**. The principles of **Animalism** are being left behind.

KEY CHARACTER: SNOWBALL AS SCAPEGOAT (A01)

Snowball's exile provides Napoleon with a scapegoat – if any of Napoleon's plans fail, Snowball can always be blamed. (A scapegoat unites people against a common enemy.)

Napoleon tells the animals that the windmill was not destroyed by the storm but was sabotaged by Snowball and shows them the 'evidence' of Snowball's footprints. The animals believe that Napoleon is the only one who can protect them from the outside world.

KEY CONTEXT (A03)

Hitler used the Jews as scapegoats for Germany's economic and political problems in the 1930s. Scapegoats are usually stereotyped so that they appear as inhuman as possible to those who are judging them. Think about how we see this happen to Snowball.

KEY THEME: THE LANGUAGE OF POWER (A02)

The animals' labour is said to be voluntary but it is actually compulsory: if the animals don't work, they will have their rations 'reduced by half' (p. 37). This distortion of language is one way in which the pigs control the farm animals (see **Part Four: Themes** for further examples).

REVISION FOCUS: AT A LOSS FOR WORDS

The following are examples of the close ties between language and power in the book:

● Simplification of language: Major's statement that 'Whatever goes upon two legs, is an enemy. Whatever goes upon four legs, or has wings, is a friend.' (Ch. 1, p. 6) is reduced to the slogan 'Four legs good, two legs bad' (Ch. 3, p. 21). This loss of meaning becomes dangerous when the sheep chant the slogan to drown opposition to Napoleon.

● Inarticulate opposition: Clover's inability to articulate her own feelings means that she has to resort to singing 'Beasts of England' to mark her sadness – an ineffective form of protest.

Can you find any other examples where the animals fail to articulate their opposition in this chapter? Can you link them to events later (or earlier) in the book?

> **CHECKPOINT 14** (A02)
>
> How does Squealer stop the animals from questioning Napoleon's decision to trade?

AIMING HIGH: ORWELL'S USE OF IRONY

This chapter shows the gradual but definite grasp of power by the pigs as 'the animals worked like slaves' (p. 37). You need to show how Orwell's use of irony directs our attention to what is really happening. For example, you could comment that the animals' pride that their work is 'for the benefit of themselves' and not for 'idle, thieving human beings' (p. 37) is undercut by our awareness that the animals are being exploited in exactly this way by the pigs.

KEY QUOTATION: ORWELL'S USE OF LANGUAGE (A02)

When the pigs move into the farmhouse, the animals feel uneasy: 'Again the animals seemed to remember that a resolution against this had been passed in the early days, and again Squealer was able to convince them that this was not the case.' (p. 42)

Orwell's use of the linking verb 'seemed' rather than stating more definitely that 'the animals remembered' shows us that the animals don't trust their own memories – and how easily they accept Squealer's explanation.

CHAPTER 7: TERROR

SUMMARY

- The animals face starvation.
- The windmill is rebuilt (with thicker walls) but work is slow.
- In order to hide the shortage of food on the farm from the outside world, Napoleon ensures that Mr Whymper, his solicitor, sees bins that are apparently full of grain and meal.
- The hens, angry that their eggs are being sold to Whymper, rebel.
- Napoleon decides to sell some timber and conducts separate negotiations with Mr Pilkington and Mr Frederick.
- Four pigs and three hens, among others, are executed in front of the other terrified animals.

CHECKPOINT 15 (A02)

How does Orwell describe the executions and what effect does this have?

WHY IS THIS CHAPTER IMPORTANT?

A The **terrible weather** mentioned at the start of the chapter reinforces the **harsh realities** of life for the animals.

B Deceitful Napoleon **tricks** the other farmers into believing that the animals are happy and contented and that food is plentiful.

C The hens' refusal to hand over their eggs for sale forms the first serious internal **challenge** to Napoleon's power.

D Napoleon decides to sell some timber and conducts **negotiations** with Mr Pilkington and Mr Frederick but never both at the same time.

E The pigs feel confident enough to **rewrite history**, telling the animals that Snowball was a **coward** at the Battle of the Cowshed.

F The executions that Napoleon organises parallel Stalin's violent **elimination** of his opponents during the 1920s and 1930s (see **Part Four: Themes**). Napoleon's **cruelty** is emphasised by his disproportionately **brutal** and **unexpected** violence.

TOP TIP (A02)

After the executions, notice that Orwell shifts from his use of the third person narrative to Clover's unspoken thoughts and feelings. What effect does this have on the reader? Think about why Orwell does this.

KEY THEME: LANGUAGE AND POWER (A02)

After the executions, Clover can't think or voice her objections to what has just happened. She still trusts the pigs – showing how successfully the pigs have brainwashed the animals. All Clover can do, as she 'lacked the words' (p. 55) to protest, is sing 'Beasts of England'. The song becomes a substitute for language and is then banned because its references to a better world could be seen as subversive. It is replaced with Minimus's worthless anthem.

KEY THEME: TYRANNY AND TERROR (A02)

We can clearly see how successful Napoleon's and Squealer's techniques are: the condemned animals confess to non-existent crimes. Almost as horrifying as the executions is the fact that although the farm animals are terrified by the slaughter, they believe that the victims were traitors.

We see other techniques in this chapter: supposed sabotage is used again as a pretext by Napoleon to remove his opposition. His tactics also point up the gullibility of the animals; for example, when Napoleon appears to be about to sell the timber to Pilkington, the animals are told that Snowball is living on Frederick's farm. When he negotiates with Frederick, Snowball is said to be living with Pilkington.

TOP TIP: WRITING ABOUT NAPOLEON (A02)

Look at how our view of Napoleon changes in this chapter: Napoleon is now rarely seen in public and is referred to as 'Our Leader, Comrade Napoleon' (p. 51). Squealer creates an image of Napoleon as a wise, heroic leader: Napoleon is said to be a brave and successful fighter. He awards himself medals and his appearances become mainly ceremonial.

You could comment on the fact that Squealer becomes more and more important as the only means of communication between Napoleon and the other animals. Even the most stupid of the animals question the executions but Squealer is again able to answer them. The animals' trust in the pigs is another reason for Napoleon's success.

AIMING HIGH: WRITING ABOUT ORWELL'S USE OF LANGUAGE ⭐

Note how the detailed description of the farm and the emphasis on its beauty on 'a clear spring evening' (p. 54) is used by Orwell to create an image of what the animals have lost and how the revolution could have turned out. He juxtaposes two different visions in this chapter: the ideal of the freedom and peace that the animals could have achieved is set against the awful reality of their lives. We are reminded of what the revolution originally set out to do and how its ideals have been destroyed by the pigs. How does Orwell's sentence structure change here? What effect does it create?

It is a good idea to compare this passage to the 'new dawn' passage in Chapter 2 (p. 13). How do the animals react to the farm in these two extracts? What point is Orwell making?

CHECKPOINT 16 (A01)

Does Napoleon deserve his medals? Why does he award them to himself and what does this show?

TOP TIP (A01)

Make careful notes on the differences between Squealer's account of the Battle of the Cowshed and what we are told on pages 25–6. What aspects are diminished? What aspects are invented?

CHAPTER 8: THE BATTLE OF THE WINDMILL

SUMMARY

- It is clear that the Seven Commandments are being altered.
- The animals are working even harder and eating less than they were under Mr Jones.
- The windmill is finished.
- Napoleon finally sells the timber to Frederick, who pays with forged notes. When he realises that Frederick has tricked him, Napoleon passes the death sentence on the farmer.
- Frederick then invades the farm and destroys the windmill. The Battle of the Windmill is won by the animals but only just.
- The pigs find a crate of whisky and break the Fifth Commandment, rewriting it to accommodate their actions.

TOP TIP (A01)

Compare the Battle of the Windmill to the description of the Battle of the Cowshed in Chapter 4. Which is the harder battle? Why?

WHY IS THIS CHAPTER IMPORTANT?

A Napoleon's **abuse** of **power** becomes more **blatant**. Any animals who **defy** him are **slaughtered**, the rest are **terrified** by his dogs.

B Orwell reminds us that the animals' lives are **worsening** under Napoleon. Following the aftermath of the **executions**, the dogs are a **threatening** presence on the farm and the animals face daily **hardships**.

C Napoleon now lives in even greater **comfort**, and seems to ignore Major's assertion that 'All the habits of Man are evil' (Ch. 1, p. 6).

D The animals are left **demoralised** at the end of this chapter as the building of the windmill proves to be **futile**.

E Squealer's **statistics** bear no relation to the food that the animals are given, highlighting the gap between his **lies** and **reality**.

KEY LANGUAGE: ORWELL'S IRONIC NARRATOR (A02)

From the animals' viewpoint, the discovery of Squealer, lying with a pot of paint and a brush at the foot of the wall, is a 'strange incident which hardly anyone was able to understand' (p. 68). To us, it is clear that Squealer alters the Commandments as the pigs break them – he is literally rewriting history. This episode is a good example of Orwell's use of the narrator to create irony.

KEY THEME: EXPLOITATION (A01)

Squealer is caught red-handed altering the Commandments, yet the animals still don't see what is happening to them; they don't even trust the evidence of their own eyes. The animals are so used to having others think for them that they can't think for themselves. The pigs' confidence in their own power means that they make fewer efforts to cover their tracks.

AIMING HIGH: DOUBLETHINK

In Orwell's final novel *Nineteen Eighty-Four*, IngSoc, the totalitarian regime, uses 'doublethink' to control the behaviour of its people, by removing their freedom to think for themselves. Can you see any similarities between the techniques used by IngSoc in *Nineteen Eighty-Four* and the pigs in *Animal Farm*? What does this tell you about Orwell's concerns and his motivation for writing these books? (Remember that if you mention other works by Orwell, you have to show how they relate to *Animal Farm*.)

TOP TIP: WRITING ABOUT THE BATTLE OF THE WINDMILL   (A02)

The Battle of the Windmill is one of the few times when we see the animals fighting for a common cause. You should show how their actions contrast sharply with those at the Battle of the Cowshed   and note that the pain and effort involved in this later battle are stressed by Orwell. Look at how Squealer completely misrepresents the Battle of the Windmill. Why does he do this? How is he able to get away with it?

TOP TIP   (A01)

When writing about the Battle of the Windmill, compare the differences in leadership between Snowball and Napoleon in the two battles.

REVISION FOCUS: DICTATORS AND POWER

How do you think dictators keep power? Think about:

- The removal of democracy: the abolition of debates and elections removes a valuable way for the animals to express their opinions.
- Terror: the bloodbath in the barn and the executions that follow remind us of the most primitive way of maintaining power – terror.
- The control of information: all information is carefully managed by the pigs to hide their real aims. The lack of any other source of information means that the animals have no way of checking the truth.
- Propaganda: Napoleon uses Squealer's abilities to 'turn black into white' (Ch. 1, p. 9) to brainwash the farm animals into accepting his decisions and actions.

Can you think of any other methods used in the text?

Remember that throughout your answer you need to show your reader how Napoleon's rise to power relates to Orwell's purpose in writing the book. It's an explicitly political text and he wants his message to the reader to be as clear as possible. Make sure you explain to *your* reader why Orwell presents Napoleon as he does.

CHAPTER 9: BOXER IS BETRAYED

SUMMARY

- Boxer's hoof takes a long time to heal but he refuses to work any less.
- Life on the farm is very hard: the animals are starving as rations have been reduced even further.
- The young pigs are to be educated in a separate schoolroom.
- Moses returns to the farm.
- Boxer collapses in the quarry and is sold by the pigs to the owners of the knacker's yard.
- The pigs buy another crate of whisky and have a memorial banquet for Boxer.

WHY IS THIS CHAPTER IMPORTANT?

A The talk about the use of an area of pasture for retired animals shows how much the animals now rely on **rumour** rather than **fact**.

B The farm's **inequality** is clear in the **comparison** between the hungry and cold animals, whose lives are 'harsh and bare' (p. 70) and the pigs who 'were putting on weight if anything' (p. 71).

C Moses returns to the farm with tales of 'Sugarcandy Mountain' (p. 73), showing that the animals again have to resort to the **hope** of an **afterlife** rather than face the **realities** of their lives.

D We also realise how much Boxer has **sacrificed** for the revolution.

E Major's **prophecy** of Boxer's end is **fulfilled** – though in a far worse way than he predicted.

TOP TIP (A03)

At the start, Moses is seen to be Mr Jones's pet – a parallel of the relationship between the Russian Orthodox Church and the Tsar. Why do the pigs allow Moses to return?

CHECKPOINT 17 (A02)

Does the reference to the pigs' tails on page 71 of the text remind you of anything earlier in the story? What point is being reinforced here?

KEY THEME: PROPAGANDA (A02)

The pigs divert attention from the animals' hard lives and the inequality on the farm through the use of parades, songs and propaganda. Squealer also uses words in ways that completely contradict their meaning, such as the 'Spontaneous Demonstration' (p. 72), which is carefully organised, and the 'Republic' (p. 73) which has only one candidate for election: Napoleon. When the animals' rations have to be reduced, Squealer refers to the change 'as a "readjustment", never as a "reduction"' (p. 70).

KEY STRUCTURE: BACK TO THE FUTURE? (A02)

The piglets are trained to continue the pigs' dominance over the other animals. The prospects for the future look bleak as, even if Napoleon were to die, other pigs are ready to assume leadership. The return of Moses suggests that the other animals are, at best, back where they started.

KEY CHARACTER: BOXER (A01)

Boxer's death is the emotional climax of the book (more so than the executions) and provides another significant moment in the story. It is one of the first times we see Benjamin's devotion to his friend but we also realise what the revolution has cost Boxer, who has sacrificed his health – and life – for the success of Animal Farm.

The animals' inability to help Boxer until it is too late suggests that this would never have happened if they had been more involved at the start of the revolution instead of relying on the pigs to take control. Orwell shows us that the farm animals' blind faith in the pigs and their inability to oppose them has terrible consequences.

AIMING HIGH: WRITING ABOUT BOXER'S DEATH ⭐

Boxer's slaughter at the hands of the knacker is the most powerful event in *Animal Farm*, showing us how the pigs have betrayed the animals' trust. Look at how the pigs' indifference to Boxer emphasises their ruthlessness. What is the reader meant to think about the fact that while the animals are starving, the pigs have a banquet? Where does Orwell suggest the money for this has come from? Take careful note of the language Orwell uses at this point. You could explore how it differs from the language Orwell uses during the executions.

CHECKPOINT 18 (A01)

A republic is a country that elects its leaders and where the head of government is not a monarch. Do you think that Animal Farm is a republic?

TOP TIP (A02)

Look at how often the word 'slave' is used in this chapter. What effect does it have on the reader?

CHAPTER 10: FULL CIRCLE?

SUMMARY

- Many years have passed. Few of the old animals still survive; the younger ones don't understand Animalism.
- The windmill has been restored and another one is being built.
- Although the farm is richer, the animals work harder than ever. Napoleon now has complete control over the other animals.
- Clover is horrified to see the pigs walking on their hind legs and Napoleon carrying a whip.
- The Commandments have been erased from the barn wall and replaced by a single slogan (see **Key quotation**).
- The pigs wear clothes, smoke and read newspapers.
- The pigs invite the farmers to dinner.
- The animals are appalled that they can no longer distinguish between the faces of the humans and the pigs. The pigs' transformation is complete.

KEY CONTEXT (A03)

The closing scene in the book was inspired by the Tehran Conference of 1943 and the meeting of Stalin, Roosevelt and Churchill as allies. Orwell predicted that peace between them would be fragile – as demonstrated when Napoleon and the farmers cheat at cards.

WHY IS THIS CHAPTER IMPORTANT?

A The only animals who seem to **profit** from the farm are the **pigs**.

B Despite the fact that none of the benefits they had expected have arrived, the animals still **hope** that some day they will be free.

C The **removal** of the Seven Commandments and the imposition of a single **nonsensical** slogan show how thoroughly the revolution has been **corrupted**.

D Major's hopes of a **free** and **equal** society are seen to be just as he described them – a 'dream' (Ch. 1, p. 3).

E The fact that Napoleon carries a **whip** – seen at the opening of the book as a **symbol** of man's vicious **oppression** – suggests that a **violent** future lies ahead.

F We see that the revolution has brought the animals **back to where they started** – they have only changed masters.

CHECKPOINT 19 (A01)

Napoleon states that 'The truest happiness ... lay in working hard and living frugally' (p. 81). In what ways do the pigs fail to live up to this?

KEY STRUCTURE: PARALLELS AND MEANING (A02)

Much of the impact of this chapter is created through parallels with the start of the story. The sheep now bleat 'Four legs good. Two legs *better*' (p. 84), showing how an unthinking mob can prop up a tyrant.

After Boxer's death, the pigs' adoption of human behaviour is rapid. Clover's horrified neighing when she sees Squealer walking on his hind legs highlights the shock at what has gradually happened to the animals. The arrival of humans on the farm emphasises the complete overthrow of every one of Major's instructions.

KEY QUOTATION: SIMPLIFYING LANGUAGE (A02)

The Seven Commandments are reduced at the end of the story to one single maxim: 'ALL ANIMALS ARE EQUAL BUT SOME ANIMALS ARE MORE EQUAL THAN OTHERS' (p. 85). This slogan is oxymoronic (it is impossible to be 'more equal'). It shows us how the pigs manipulate language to distort the reality of life on the farm. Who do you think the phrase 'SOME ANIMALS' refers to?

> **TOP TIP** (A02)
>
> You might want to comment on the fact that the final, single Commandment appears entirely in capital letters. Think about the effect this has on the reader.

KEY THEME: INHUMAN LEADERS (A01)

Far from having nothing to do with man, as Major ordered, the pigs have actually surpassed man, as is clear when Mr Pilkington congratulates Napoleon on managing to run a farm in a crueller way than he does – and Napoleon says that further restrictions are planned. The pigs have systematically violated the Commandments while claiming to support the revolution and have abused the animals' trust, leaving the animals in a worse position than at the start of the book.

EXAM FOCUS: WRITING ABOUT EFFECTS (A02)

You may be asked to write about significant moments in the text. This is one reader's response, commenting on the shift to Clover's viewpoint:

This answer shows understanding of Orwell's techniques

We see the final scene in the book through Clover's eyes. Orwell often uses Clover's viewpoint and a shift in tone to give us an insight into a significant moment in the text. When Clover witnesses the pigs walking on their hind legs, Orwell uses one sentence paragraphs to drive home the shock of this sight.

Good understanding of language technique and its effect on the reader

Now you try it:

This paragraph needs a sentence focusing on the effects of the language Orwell uses when Clover sees the pigs walking on their back legs. Start: *Words such as...*

PROGRESS AND REVISION CHECK

SECTION ONE: CHECK YOUR KNOWLEDGE

Answer these quick questions to test your basic knowledge of the text, its characters and events:

1. Where do the animals gather to listen to Major?

2. Name the three dogs who live on the farm at the start of the story.

3. A vote is held to decide whether or not a particular animal should be called 'comrade'. Which animal is it?

4. Name the song that Major teaches the animals.

5. What did the pigs use to teach themselves to read?

6. What is the Sixth Commandment?

7. What was the point of the Wild Comrades Re-education Committee?

8. Who is seen standing outside a public house in Willingdon?

9. Who says 'A bed merely means a place to sleep in … The rule was against *sheets*, which are a human invention'?

10. Who works by moonlight?

11. Who is allowed to get up later than the other animals?

12. Who has a death sentence placed upon them?

13. Who appears at the end of the sentence: 'Whenever anything went wrong it became usual to attribute it to …'?

14. Who casts 'a very ugly look' at Boxer?

15. Why does Napoleon gallop around the yard in a bowler hat?

16. Where did the pigs get the money to buy a second crate of whisky?

17. What part of the farm was meant to be put aside for retired animals?

18. Name the two animals who read the final single Commandment.

19. Who is seen with a pipe in his mouth?

20. What card do Napoleon and Mr Pilkington both produce?

PROGRESS AND REVISION CHECK

SECTION TWO: CHECK YOUR UNDERSTANDING

Here are some tasks which require slightly longer responses. In each case try to write at least three to four paragraphs.

Task 1: Compare what we see of Snowball's behaviour with what we are told about him after he flees the farm. Think about:

- What we learn about him before Chapter 5
- What we are told about him after he flees the farm

Task 2: What is the significance of the protest about the cancellation of the Sunday meetings in Chapter 5? Think about:

- Who protests and why
- How this mirrors or foreshadows other events in the text

PROGRESS CHECK

GOOD PROGRESS

I can:

- understand how Orwell has sequenced and revealed events. ☐
- refer to the importance of key events in the text. ☐
- select well-chosen evidence, including key quotations, to support my ideas. ☐

EXCELLENT PROGRESS

I can:

- refer in depth to main and minor events and how they contribute to the development of the plot. ☐
- understand how Orwell has carefully ordered or revealed events for particular effects. ☐
- draw on a range of carefully selected key evidence, including quotations, to support my ideas. ☐

WHO'S WHO?

Mr Jones

Major

Mr Pilkington & Mr Frederick

Mr Whymper

Napoleon

Squealer

Boxer

Snowball

Benjamin

Clover

Pigs

Moses

Mollie

Dogs

Muriel

Hens, geese & ducklings

Sheep

Cat

MAJOR

MAJOR'S ROLE IN THE TEXT

Major is a 'highly regarded' pig who is a natural leader. He is twelve years old and has 'a wise and benevolent appearance' (Ch. 1, p. 1). He represents both Karl Marx and Lenin in the book's allegorical representation of Russian history. In the text:

- Major's speech prophesises much of what will happen on the farm – the irony being that it happens under Napoleon, not Jones.

- Major makes a passionate speech that is a mix of Marxism and Leninism. This is the political underpinning of the book – a socialist view of life as a struggle against tyranny, and the need to strive for a free and equal society.

- Major's speech is vital. Orwell uses it to establish at the start of the book the hope of an equal, just society – one that we agree with. This also provides the standard by which we judge the farm following the revolution, as we see when Major predicts Boxer's fate.

- the pigs develop Major's ideas and then pervert them, as Orwell believed Stalin took socialist ideas and twisted them for his own benefit.

- in Chapter 10, Napoleon states that the animals should no longer march past Major's skull, highlighting the gulf between Major's aims and the reality of life under Napoleon.

TOP TIP **A02**

Remember that Orwell uses Major to present complex political ideas to his readers in a readable, easily understood way.

TOP TIP: WRITING ABOUT MAJOR **A02**

Orwell wrote *Animal Farm* to make a particular political point. Show how Major is central to this: his (and Karl Marx's) ideas form the philosophical and political heart of the story. When writing about Major's speech, explain how Orwell presents his ideas, the techniques he uses (such as assertion, rhetorical questions and repetition) and the effect this has on the reader.

Marx   Lenin

SNOWBALL

SNOWBALL'S ROLE IN THE TEXT

Snowball is the farm's intellectual. He helps to plan the revolution and rivals Napoleon for leadership of Animal Farm. In the text, Snowball:

- energetically promotes the revolution and teaches the animals new skills.
- appears to care for the wellbeing of the other animals, but also supports Napoleon's seizure of the apples.
- is brave in battle and a brilliant strategist. He is the mastermind behind the victorious Battle of the Cowshed, as well as the windmill.
- for all his brilliance, does not notice Napoleon's steady climb to power – or the use he makes of the dogs.
- is nearly killed by Napoleon's dogs in Chapter 5 and flees from the farm.
- after his expulsion, is used as a scapegoat for any misfortune on the farm. He is also used as a malign threat, to frighten the animals into obedience.

SNOWBALL'S IMPORTANCE TO THE TEXT AS A WHOLE

TOP TIP (A01)

Snowball is generally presented positively in the story. It is also useful to identify negative descriptions or examples of his behaviour (for example, he is said to lack Napoleon's 'depth of character' Ch. 2, p. 9).

Snowball represents Leon Trotsky, one of the leading figures of the Russian Revolution, who led the Red Army to victory in the Russian Civil War. Orwell presents him as a brilliant idealist, who attempts to modernise society. He uses Snowball to show us an alternative leader to Napoleon: Snowball is intellectual, 'indefatigable' (Ch. 3, p. 19) in organising the other animals into committees and full of 'plans for innovations and improvements' (Ch. 5, p. 30), such as the windmill. He also uses democratic processes such as meetings and committees to put forward his ideas – although he too agrees that the apples and milk should be kept for the pigs, raising the question of exactly how equal a society under Snowball would have been.

EXAM FOCUS: WRITING ABOUT SNOWBALL (A01)

Key point	Evidence/Further meaning
• Snowball is seen as charismatic and a brilliant thinker and communicator.	• 'Snowball was … quicker in speech and more inventive.' (Ch. 2, p. 9)
• Snowball is dedicated to spreading Major's revolutionary ideas and teaching the animals to run the farm themselves.	• 'He formed the Egg Production Committee … the Clean Tails League … the Wild Comrades' Re-education Committee.' (Ch. 3, p. 19) The comic nature of his committees suggests that his approach is theoretical and impractical – and likely to fail.
• Snowball is the first to simplify language on Animal Farm.	• 'Four legs good, two legs bad.' (Ch. 3, p. 21)
• Snowball's ruthlessness makes us wonder how different the revolution would have been under him.	• 'The only good human being is a dead one.' (Ch. 4, p. 26)

TOP TIP: WRITING ABOUT SNOWBALL (A01)

You might be asked to contrast Snowball's character with Napoleon's. You could begin by examining Chapter 2, where the two characters are explicitly linked by Orwell: Snowball's plans and ideals seem to put Napoleon in the shade. In contrast to the more talkative Snowball, Napoleon is relatively silent but equally ambitious. Napoleon and Snowball have differing ideas about Animalism – their disagreements parallel those of Stalin and Trotsky (see **Part Four: Themes**).

When writing, compare the two characters' reactions to educating the animals, the Battle of the Cowshed, the Battle of the Windmill and spreading the revolution to neighbouring farms. Ask yourself how sympathetic Orwell expects us to be towards Snowball. Do you think he would have been a better leader simply because Napoleon is such a tyrant? Or can you find evidence to suggest that the animals would genuinely have been better off under Snowball? You should also focus on the way Snowball is used by Napoleon to terrorise the farm animals after he flees the farm.

Look at Snowball's reaction in Chapter 4 when the windfall apples are taken and the fact that he agrees with the pigs' use of the milk. The animals, who believe that they are all living as equals, 'had assumed as a matter of course' (p. 21) that the windfall apples would be shared out, along with the milk. Orwell tells us that, despite the murmured protests of the animals, 'it was no use' (p. 22) as all the pigs are in agreement. For Orwell this was one of the central passages in the book. Even Mr Jones put the milk in the hens' mash rather than keep it for himself.

> **TOP TIP** (A01)
>
> When writing about a character, try to explain their function in the story.

NAPOLEON

NAPOLEON'S ROLE IN THE TEXT

Napoleon is the pig who seizes control of Animal Farm after Mr Jones is expelled. Based on Joseph Stalin, he systematically destroys all of Major's ideals as he gradually adopts the behaviour and vices of the humans that Major had criticised. He becomes a dictator. In the text, Napoleon:

- takes control of the food supply immediately after the revolution to get the animals' support.
- removes the puppies and expels Snowball, demonstrating for the first time the extent of his power.
- does not participate in the Battle of the Cowshed but later rewrites history to portray himself as a heroic leader.
- uses Squealer to control the animals and disguise his rise to power.
- shows his cruelty at several points – particularly in his treatment of Boxer.
- becomes more selfish as the story progresses – or at least less concerned with hiding his selfishness. By the end of the story, he has almost entirely taken the place of Mr Jones – although he is worse because he has betrayed the revolution and the animals on the farm.
- blames Snowball for his own mistakes and creates an atmosphere of hysteria in which animals will confess to the most ludicrous crimes.

KEY CONTEXT (A03)

Orwell wrote that one of *Animal Farm*'s messages was 'that *that kind* of revolution ... led by unconsciously power-hungry people, can only lead to a change of masters.' This is why Napoleon mirrors Mr Jones (and the other humans) so closely at the end of the story.

NAPOLEON'S IMPORTANCE TO THE TEXT AS A WHOLE

Napoleon is central to Orwell's satirical purpose. He represents the nightmare of dictatorship, and Orwell uses him to demonstrate what happens when people surrender their power to someone else. Napoleon has planned his takeover for a long time (as we see when he removes the puppies from their mothers). He is underhand and secretive – and undemocratic. Orwell uses Napoleon's rise to power to show us how people become tyrants – and the tools they use to keep themselves in power, such as propaganda, fear and exploiting others' trust and stupidity. Napoleon is a thinly disguised Joseph Stalin (see photo), whose Soviet dictatorship is thought to have been responsible for the deaths of ten million people.

EXAM FOCUS: WRITING ABOUT NAPOLEON (A01)

Key point	Evidence/Further meaning
• He is single-minded and forceful.	• He is a 'fierce-looking' boar with 'a reputation for getting his own way'. (Ch. 2, p. 9) This quotation also foreshadows the brutal way in which he will seize power.
• His rise to power is premeditated – it has been carefully planned.	• Napoleon 'seemed to be biding his time'. (Ch. 5, p. 30)
• Napoleon has become a dictator, breaking Major's instructions that 'no animal must ever **tyrannize** over his own kind' and 'No animal must ever kill any other animal' (Ch. 1, p. 6).	• 'Napoleon acted swiftly and ruthlessly.' (Ch. 7, p. 48) The short sentence and simple adverbs mirror the blunt efficiency of Napoleon.
• Contrary to Major's spirit of equality, Napoleon separates himself from the other animals, sleeps in the farmhouse (breaking another of the Commandments) and resorts to intimidation.	• 'Napoleon rarely appeared in public, but spent all his time in the farmhouse, which was guarded at each door by fierce-looking dogs.' (Ch. 7, p. 47)
• Napoleon inverts the true meaning of Animalism. He is a hypocrite, claiming animals should live frugally while he lives in luxury.	• 'Napoleon had denounced such ideas as contrary to the spirit of Animalism. The truest happiness, he said, lay in working hard and living frugally.' (Ch. 10, p. 81)

TOP TIP: WRITING ABOUT NAPOLEON (A01)

When writing about Napoleon, make sure that you show how he uses the revolution for his own gain: look at his increasing preoccupation with his position and status. Look at how he manipulates events to gain control: show how the Seven Commandments are rewritten throughout the story to suit Napoleon's aims, and how Squealer announces his intentions to the animals (who are terrified into silent agreement) when it is clear that his plans have already been made. You could also discuss how Orwell presents Napoleon gradually distancing himself from the other animals (dining from Crown Derby china, eating sugar and drinking alcohol) and staging elaborate ceremonies in his own honour. At what point do you think Napoleon becomes a tyrant?

KEY CONTEXT (A03)

Napoleon Bonaparte was the name of the revolutionary who became Emperor of France in 1804.

SQUEALER

SQUEALER'S ROLE IN THE TEXT

Squealer is Napoleon's propagandist, his spin doctor, who justifies Napoleon's seizure of power. In the text, Squealer:

- is responsible for the devious changes to the Commandments.
- confuses the animals and makes them doubt their own memories, persuading them that he is right.
- gives the animals meaningless lists of statistics to convince them that life under Napoleon is getting better.
- uses his own eloquence and Napoleon's brutal dogs to enforce Napoleon's message.
- grows fatter as the story progresses, as he benefits from working for Napoleon.

SQUEALER'S IMPORTANCE TO THE TEXT AS A WHOLE

Orwell uses Squealer to demonstrate how politicians use language and propaganda to control people, a theme he develops in *Nineteen Eighty-Four*. Squealer's 'twinkling eyes', 'shrill voice' and other mannerisms (Ch. 2, p. 9) emphasise the persuasiveness of this character. He is like the modern spin doctor, presenting events and ideas in the form that best suits Napoleon's aims.

The sinister side to Squealer's character is apparent when he is seen noting the signs of resistance to Napoleon – even when these arrive in the form of gentle questions from characters such as Boxer. His ugly sideways looks and the subsequent attack on Boxer suggest that Squealer's propaganda is more sinister than simply ensuring that the animals obey Napoleon: it is also used to eliminate anyone who doubts him. Squealer's arrogance and contempt for the other animals show the dismissive attitude that the propagandist has towards those he exploits.

TOP TIP (A01)

When writing about Squealer, note that he doesn't rely on the power of words alone. When do we first realise that the dogs are accompanying him around the farm?

EXAM FOCUS: WRITING ABOUT SQUEALER (A01)

Key point	Evidence/Further meaning
• Squealer is very persuasive. The animals are easily convinced by his explanations and arguments.	• We are told that he is a 'brilliant talker' who can 'turn black into white' (Ch. 2, p. 9).
• Squealer is a coward.	• He is 'unaccountably ... absent' (Ch. 8, p. 66) from the fighting.
• He convinces the animals that Napoleon is acting in their best interests despite the fact that Napoleon is doing the very opposite.	• 'No one believes more firmly than Comrade Napoleon that all animals are equal ... But sometimes you might make the wrong decisions, comrades, and then where would we be?' (Ch. 4, p. 35)
• Squealer uses emotion to manipulate the animals.	• '"It was the most affecting sight I have ever seen!", said Squealer, lifting a trotter and wiping away a tear.' (Ch. 9, p. 78)
• The way in which Squealer looks at Boxer – and the attack on him that follows – highlights the sinister side to Squealer's character.	• 'he cast a very ugly look at Boxer' (Ch. 7, p. 51) Squealer's role is to ensure that any opposition to Napoleon is eliminated.

AIMING HIGH: WRITING ABOUT SQUEALER

The relationship between language and power was something Orwell saw as very important – it is a theme in his novel *Nineteen Eighty-Four* – and he wrote several influential essays on the subject. Squealer is therefore a particularly significant character in the book, as he reflects Orwell's wider concerns with how language can be misused to exploit people.

When writing about Squealer, you must explain to your reader the techniques that Squealer uses to control the flow of information to the animals: look at how he changes the Commandments on the wall, the lists of figures he uses to baffle the starving animals and how he rewrites history (his changing interpretations of the Battle of the Cowshed, for example). Ask yourself why Squealer is so successful. Does he rely only on the power of speech?

TOP TIP (A02)

Notice how Squealer physically changes as the story progresses. Think about why Orwell mentions this and how the pigs look at the end of the book.

BOXER

BOXER'S ROLE IN THE TEXT

Boxer the carthorse is 'an enormous beast' (Ch. 1, p. 2), the revolution's most loyal disciple who is prepared to make huge sacrifices for the farm's success. He represents the proletariat and their hopes for a better world. In the text, Boxer:

- is a loyal supporter of the revolution. He passes on the pigs' teachings to the other animals and is 'unfailing' (Ch. 2, p. 10) in his attendance at the farm meetings.
- shows his dedication to the revolution by his surrender of the hat he uses to protect himself from flies, unlike Mollie who holds on to her ribbons.
- has strength and total commitment, which are vital to the success of the harvest – and the revolution.
- shows his integrity and honesty by his defence of Snowball, which marks him out to Squealer. His strength saves him from the dogs when they attack him at the show trial.
- insists on working until he sees the windmill rebuilt.
- believes the pigs' promises of a happy retirement but is sold to the knacker (or slaughterhouse).

TOP TIP (A01)

Notice how Boxer's gentleness and kindness are emphasised when we first see him. Orwell intends us to see him as a sympathetic and heroic character.

BOXER'S IMPORTANCE TO THE TEXT AS A WHOLE (A01)

Orwell presents Boxer as a kind, selfless, heroic figure. As readers we care about Boxer because he is presented sympathetically: he is a loyal and dedicated follower of Napoleon, even though he does not fully understand the ideas behind the revolution. His lack of intelligence and unquestioning trust in the pigs mean that he is vulnerable to their exploitation. This does not just result in suffering: Orwell uses him to make the point that such behaviour is fatal. Boxer's death demonstrates Napoleon's cruelty and how far the dictator will go to exploit someone – emphasising how similar Napoleon has become to Jones. (Do you remember what Major says will happen to Boxer under Jones?) The pigs toast Boxer with whisky – forbidden by Major – which has been bought with the proceeds of his death. Even in death, Orwell shows us, Boxer is exploited by the pigs.

EXAM FOCUS: WRITING ABOUT BOXER   **A01**

Key point	Evidence/Further meaning
Major's words prove prophetic for Boxer – though the irony is that he is sent to his death by Napoleon rather than Mr Jones.	'You, Boxer, the very day that those great muscles of yours lose their power, Jones will send you to the knacker, who will cut your throat and boil you down for the fox-hounds.' (Ch. 1, p. 5)
Even when he is being driven to the knacker's yard, Boxer has to be told what is happening to him.	'"Boxer!" cried Clover in a terrible voice. "Boxer! Get out! Get out quickly! They are taking you to your death!"' (Ch. 9, p. 77)
For all his 'terrifying' (Ch. 4, p. 26) fighting during the Battle of the Cowshed, Boxer's compassion and humility are also apparent. He is devastated when he thinks he has killed the stable-lad and makes it clear that he does not want to kill even his worst enemy.	'"I have no wish to take life, not even human life," repeated Boxer, and his eyes were full of tears.' (Ch. 4, p. 26) Boxer's brave, gentle nature is used by Orwell as a contrast to Napoleon's cowardly thuggery.
Boxer lacks intelligence. He can't learn to read beyond 'A, B, C, D' although he tries with 'all his might' (Ch. 3, p. 20) to do so.	'Boxer could not get beyond the letter D.' (Ch. 3, p. 20) The consequences of a lack of literacy are made explicit by Boxer's fate.
Boxer's blind faith in the pigs is disastrous. Even after the dogs attack him and he sees the massacre of the animals on the farm, Boxer (who is upset by what he has seen) does not blame the pigs, and decides to work harder.	'It must be due to some fault in ourselves.' (Ch. 7, p. 54) Boxer cannot recognise the pigs' corruption – another reason for Napoleon's success in his quest for power.

AIMING HIGH: BOXER, OUR HERO?

Orwell presents Boxer as the most heroic animal in the story. When writing about Boxer, you can compare how he is shown to us on different occasions: in the barn, at the Battle of the Cowshed, building the windmill. Explain what techniques Orwell uses to make him so sympathetic. Would we care so much about the events in Chapter 9 without these earlier events? Ask yourself which animals on the farm are given the most attention by Orwell in the story. Why does Orwell focus on this character rather than, say, one of the sheep? Who do you think Orwell expects us to side with? How is this linked to his reason for writing the book?

TOP TIP   **A02**

Boxer's death is the emotional climax of the book. Make careful notes on the language Orwell uses at this point and the effect this has on the reader.

CLOVER

CLOVER'S ROLE IN THE TEXT

Like Boxer, Clover represents the proletariat. Clover is a loyal disciple of the Animalist revolution, right to the end of the story. She criticises Mollie for her betrayal of Major's ideals. In the text, Clover:

- is the only character whose thoughts we are given in detail.
- is not as strong as Boxer, but is slightly more intelligent (she can read better than he can).
- checks the Commandments as the pigs take control of the farm but never acts upon her doubts.
- trusts the pigs and doubts her own memory. Her obedient nature is easily exploited by Squealer. Even after the executions she is still loyal to Napoleon.
- sees the pigs walking on their hind legs and the farmers playing cards with Napoleon.

AIMING HIGH: WRITING ABOUT CLOVER

When writing about Clover, discuss how Orwell uses Clover's journey in the story to show how ordinary people can lose their freedom in small steps. We are meant to sympathise with her: she is a kind, protective figure in the story, as we see in her treatment of the ducklings and of Boxer when he is injured. You should point out that we see events at the end of the book and the aftermath of the executions through Clover's eyes. These are the only times when he shifts from the detached view of his narrator.

Ask yourself why Orwell makes Clover one of the only characters to survive to the end of the story. How has she changed from the start of the book? Do you think her journey mirrors that of the farm in any way?

TOP TIP (A02)

Look at the ways in which Orwell ensures that we identify with Clover from the start of the story. Why does he choose her to witness the pigs' final betrayal of the animals?

BENJAMIN

BENJAMIN'S ROLE IN THE TEXT

Benjamin the donkey is introduced as 'the oldest animal on the farm, and the worst tempered' (Ch. 1, p. 2). Orwell uses Benjamin to show what happens to those who see wrongdoing but do nothing to stop it. In the text, Benjamin:

- unlike the rest of the animals, questions whether the animals really will be better off as a result of the revolution.
- is in the thick of the fighting at the Battle of the Cowshed.
- repeatedly refuses to read the Commandments, believing that it will create trouble.
- refuses to interfere when he sees the pigs' wrongdoing.
- alerts the others when Boxer is driven to his death – but by that stage it is too late to help.
- is outside the farmhouse with Clover when the true extent of the pigs' betrayal is revealed.

AIMING HIGH: WRITING ABOUT BENJAMIN

Orwell presents Benjamin to us as a cynical, detached character. He is dismissive of the pigs' attempts to teach the animals to read and refuses to express an opinion about the revolution. When writing about Benjamin, you should also note that he is perhaps not as isolated as Orwell suggests: he is 'devoted to Boxer' (Ch. 1, p. 2) and is one of his closest companions. What does this tell us about him? Why does Orwell give this character sympathetic traits?

TOP TIP   A02

It is useful to note the moments in the story when Benjamin understands what is happening on the farm (such as when he warns the other animals that Frederick is about to blow up the windmill).

MR JONES

Mr Jones is the farmer who owns Manor Farm but is incapable of running it. He represents the Tsar, as well as demonstrating how capitalists exploit the working classes. His cruelty is stressed in Major's speech, and the thoughtless nature of his violence is apparent in his random shooting to quell the noise from the barn. In the text, he:

- complains about the revolution in the pub, after it is over.
- tries to recapture the farm but is humiliated when he lands in the manure heap.
- ends up dying 'in an inebriates' home' (Ch. 10, p. 80), a pathetic character.

MOSES

As the religious connotations of his name suggest, Moses the raven represents the Russian Orthodox Church. In the text, he:

- convinces many of the animals that there is a better life on Sugarcandy Mountain.
- therefore persuades the animals to accept their sufferings as a temporary trial to be endured before they find eternal peace and happiness.

MOLLIE

Mollie, 'the foolish, pretty white mare' (Ch. 1, p. 2), represents the White Russians, who had a privileged life under the Tsar. She is not committed to the revolution as she doesn't want to lose her privileges. In the text, she:

- oversleeps, complains of 'mysterious pains' (Ch. 5, p. 28) and is workshy.
- seems fascinated and envious of the luxuries acquired by the humans and hankers after them.

MINOR CHARACTERS

THE DOGS

The dogs are the animal counterpart of Stalin's secret police. From the start, they are loyal animals. They are closely linked to the pigs, and later wag their tails at Napoleon in the same way that they had to Mr Jones. Along with the pigs, the dogs are rewarded for dealing ruthlessly with any objectors and murdering Napoleon's opposition.

THE SHEEP

The sheep represent the most stupid elements of society, the 'mob'. They are generally referred to as an anonymous group – no named individual stands out. Their understanding of the aims of the revolution is limited to mindlessly bleating out the slogan 'Four legs good, two legs bad' (Ch. 3, p. 21), and when Squealer decides to alter this, it takes them a week to learn the new version. The choice of animal is satirical as, stereotypically, sheep are seen as ignorant, easily led creatures.

THE HENS

The hens are the only group that shows any resistance to Napoleon. In his speech, Major specifically criticises the taking of the hens' eggs and demands that this inhumane practice be stopped, yet under Napoleon the hens are told to surrender their eggs. They retaliate by smashing their eggs. Napoleon's ruthless suppression of the hens demonstrates his willingness to use terror and murder to achieve his own ends.

KEY QUOTATION: SILENCING PROTEST (A02)

Orwell registers the animals' shock at seeing the pigs with whips:

'in spite of everything – in spite of their terror of the dogs, and of the habit, developed through long years, of never complaining, never criticizing, no matter what happened – they might have uttered some word of protest. But just at that moment, as though at a signal, all the sheep burst out into a tremendous bleating of –

'Four legs good, two legs *better*!' (Ch. 10, p. 84)

This quotation shows us the damage that indoctrination can do. The sheep drown out this moment of potential protest, which is prompted by seeing Napoleon with a whip in his trotter. The sheep silence the opposition throughout the story but the repetition of 'in spite of', the detailed description of how the animals have suppressed their doubt and the emphasis on the 'tremendous bleating' of the sheep makes it clear that this is a key moment.

TOP TIP (A01)

When writing about the dogs, you might want to consider how savage they are to begin with. Do you think they change much as characters over the course of the story?

KEY CONTEXT (A03)

The kulaks destroyed their own farms rather than let Stalin's government take them over. Stalin executed and exiled those peasants who opposed him.

TOP TIP (A01)

When writing about the pigs, don't forget that not all of the pigs agree with Napoleon's actions: look at the fate of the four porkers on page 52 of the text.

THE PIGS

From the beginning of the story the pigs, in general, are seen as the most intelligent and capable creatures. As a group, they understand Animalism and translate it into easy slogans for the other animals. They quickly become the decision-makers on the farm. They become an elite class, exploiting the animals and living a life of luxury that is unimaginable to the rest of the farm animals.

THE CAT

We hear very little of the cat once Napoleon is in power. She appears to represent the forces of self-interest and hypocrisy – as we see when she attempts to persuade the sparrows to read. She has as little as possible to do with the revolution, but is willing to enjoy its benefits.

MR PILKINGTON

A farmer, like Mr Jones, Mr Pilkington in the allegory represents Churchill. Like Napoleon, Mr Pilkington is keen to exploit his own workers. He is not a model farmer: Foxwood Farm is described as overgrown and neglected, while its owner enjoys fishing and hunting. In this respect, he is presented as a gentleman farmer.

MR FREDERICK

No more likeable than Mr Pilkington, Mr Frederick does at least run his farm a little better. He is a hard businessman and argumentative but shrewd. His most striking characteristic is his cruelty, which befits the fact he represents Hitler. Napoleon's efforts to trade and bargain with Mr Frederick are a misguided attempt at business as Mr Frederick tricks him. In a similar way, Hitler and Stalin's non-aggression pact was completely ignored by Hitler when he invaded Russia. This invasion was a violent and destructive one, in the same way as the attack on the windmill is seen as a demolition of all that the animals have achieved.

Winston Churchill

MRS JONES

Very little is seen of Mrs Jones in the book but when she is mentioned it is in an unfavourable light – she is either snoring or running away from the farm.

MR WHYMPER

The solicitor profits from the animals' misery and suffering – as the result of his dealings with Animal Farm he can buy himself a dogcart. He is described as 'a sly-looking little man' (Ch. 6, p. 41). Even his name sounds pathetic.

AIMING HIGH: WRITING ABOUT OTHER HUMANS

It is worth noting that none of the humans in the book are seen as attractive, appealing or trustworthy characters. The man who becomes Mollie's owner is described as 'a fat red-faced man in check breeches and gaiters' (Ch. 5, p. 29) while the man who drives Boxer to his death is described as 'a sly-looking man in a low-crowned bowler hat' (Ch. 9, p. 76) – an echo of the words used to describe Mr Whymper.

The repeated reference to the slyness of the human characters emphasises their unpleasantness and untrustworthiness. You should show that Orwell makes clear that the animals were right to rebel against Jones's cruelty.

TOP TIP A01

Look at how Napoleon makes use of Mr Whymper: not only to trade with Animal Farm but also to spread propaganda to other farms and the outside world.

PROGRESS AND REVISION CHECK

SECTION ONE: CHECK YOUR KNOWLEDGE

Answer these quick questions to test your basic knowledge of the characters:

1. Which character tricks Napoleon over the sale of some timber?
2. Which animal can 'turn black into white'?
3. Which animal reads newspapers they find on the rubbish heap?
4. Which animal treats Boxer's hoof with a poultice of herbs?
5. Who reads *One Thousand Useful Things to Do About the House*?
6. Who paints the words 'Animal Farm' on the top of the five-barred gate?
7. Who reads the final, single Commandment to Clover?
8. Which pig has a 'remarkable gift for composing songs and poems'?
9. Who sends a message to Napoleon that reads 'Serves you right'?
10. Who claims to have seen lump sugar growing on hedges?

SECTION TWO: CHECK YOUR UNDERSTANDING

This task requires more thought and a slightly longer response. Try to write at least three to four paragraphs.

Task: How does Orwell use Boxer's death to move *Animal Farm* towards its climax? Think about:

- How Boxer is presented in the story
- How Orwell uses Major's speech in Chapter 1

PROGRESS CHECK

GOOD PROGRESS

I can:
- explain the significance of the main characters in how the action develops. ☐
- refer to how they are described by Orwell and how this affects the way we see them. ☐

EXCELLENT PROGRESS

I can:
- analyse in detail how Orwell has shaped and developed characters over the course of the text. ☐
- infer key ideas, themes and issues from the ways characters and relationships are presented by Orwell. ☐

PART FOUR: THEMES, CONTEXTS AND SETTINGS

THEMES

POWER CORRUPTS

As well as acting as an **allegory** of Russian history, *Animal Farm* can also be taken as a more general analysis of power.

- Major's speech makes clear the extent of Jones's cruelty and exploitation. He says to the young porkers that 'every one of you will scream your lives out at the block within a year.' (Ch. 1, p. 5). The hens' eggs are sold for Jones's benefit.

- The link between power and violence is made from the opening of the story: Mr Jones fires shots into the night to silence the noisy animals.

- The existing power structures are shown to be rotten. Mr Frederick mistreats his animals and Mr Jones's neighbours each wonder whether they can 'somehow turn Jones's misfortune to his own advantage' (Ch. 4, p. 23).

- We see different forms of power in the story: the brutal power wielded by Jones (and later Napoleon), the wisdom and authority of Major, the physical power of Boxer and the intellectual power of the pigs.

- Once the pigs gain power, they begin to use it for their own gain: the day after the revolution the pigs keep the milk and apples for themselves.

- The other animals are too gullible and inarticulate to oppose the pigs, even though they have 'a vague uneasiness' (Ch. 6, p. 40) about what the pigs are doing.

- Orwell uses the Commandments to show us how the pigs gradually become more corrupt until they finally decree only one rule, the **oxymoronic** 'ALL ANIMALS ARE EQUAL BUT SOME ANIMALS ARE MORE EQUAL THAN OTHERS' (Ch. 10, p. 85).

EQUALITY

Major's speech establishes the idea that a perfect society is an equal one: 'Among us animals let there be perfect unity, perfect comradeship in the struggle.' (Ch. 1, p. 5). However, Orwell suggests that putting these ideals into practice is not easy.

- We see that there is natural hierarchy among the animals as they enter the barn to listen to Major's speech: the pigs sit down in front of Major.

- Some animals feel loyal to Jones and cannot imagine life without him.

- The other animals have different levels of intelligence and all (other than Benjamin) are less clever than the pigs, making them dependent on their leaders. You should explain in detail how the animals' dependence on the pigs is one of their fundamental stumbling blocks to equality.

- Orwell expects us to agree that a perfect society is an equal one. The animals achieve more when they are united, as the first successful harvest and the Battle of the Cowshed show.

THEME TRACKER (A02)

Power

- Ch. 1, pp. 3–6: Major's speech describes the animals' suffering and presents us with a vision of a fairer society.
- Ch. 5, pp. 29–30: Napoleon uses the sheep to silence Snowball.
- Ch. 7, p. 53: Napoleon murders his opposition.

THEME TRACKER (A02)

Equality

- Ch. 1, p. 5: Major's speech describes the inequality of the animals' lives.
- Ch. 2, p. 16: The pigs take the milk and apples for themselves.
- Ch. 5, p. 34: The animals are told there will be no more debates.

AIMING HIGH: MAJOR AND EQUALITY

Think about the reasons why the revolution fails. One stumbling block might be that Major never seems to comment on the differences between the animals – even when the dogs pounce on the rats and the votes that follow suggest real divisions exist. Do you think this is one reason why the revolution fails? Does Major's assumption that man is the common enemy ignore an existing hierarchy among the animals?

HOW DO DICTATORS RISE TO POWER?

THEME TRACKER (A02)

Rise to power

- Ch. 5, p. 34: Napoleon's dogs drive Snowball from the farm.
- Ch. 7, p. 48: Snowball is said to be visiting and sabotaging the farm at night.
- Ch. 10, p. 84: Napoleon carries a whip in his trotter.

Napoleon soon emerges as the farm's leader. His is a slow descent into tyranny. He is driven by power and throughout the book we see him plan to secure his hold on the farm and the other animals.

- Napoleon uses terror to seize power. When Snowball is driven from the farm, the animals are left 'Silent and terrified' (Ch. 5, p. 33). Squealer is then used to keep control of the animals and manipulate the flow of information to them.
- Dictators often rewrite history to produce a more flattering account of the past. Squealer completely rewrites the Battle of the Cowshed to glorify Napoleon's supposed bravery and vilify Snowball.
- The animals have to depend on their own memories, which (as a result of Squealer's rewriting of the Commandments and history itself) become less and less reliable, as we see when Clover asks Muriel to help her read the Sixth Commandment.
- Napoleon creates a 'cult of personality'. He calls himself President, awards himself medals, has a bodyguard and food tester and demands that the animals routinely praise his leadership with 'Spontaneous Demonstrations' (Ch. 9, p. 72).
- Dictators can harness mobs to drown out opposition – as the sheep do when it looks as though the animals will protest against Napoleon's decision to end the Sunday meetings.
- Napoleon's dogs demonstrate how terror can be used to suppress dissent and keep a population subjugated: 'Squealer spoke so persuasively, and the three dogs who happened to be with him growled so threateningly, that they accepted his explanation without further questions' (Ch. 5, p. 37).

KEY QUOTATION: CREATING A CLIMATE OF FEAR (A01)

Napoleon creates external enemies to gain control over the animals:

'It was noticed that whenever he seemed on the point of coming to an agreement with Frederick, Snowball was declared to be hiding at Foxwood, while, when he inclined towards Pilkington, Snowball was said to be at Pinchfield.' (Ch. 7, p. 48)

Snowball is blamed for anything that goes wrong on the farm and is said to be visiting it at night and performing 'all kinds of mischief' (Ch. 7, p. 48). Napoleon then exploits Mr Pilkington and Mr Frederick in a similar way. This extract also suggests that it is easy to persuade the animals to switch allegiance.

EDUCATION AND LEARNING

There is a **proverbial** saying that 'knowledge is power'. The pigs are clearly the most intelligent animals on the farm and soon take control.

- At first the pigs support the revolution by teaching its ideas to the other animals. As most of the farm animals cannot remember Major's speech and his ideas clearly, the pigs simplify them into seven **slogans** or Commandments.
- Snowball tries to teach the other animals to read and write.
- The pigs gradually take advantage of the other animals, instead of leading and helping them, for example when they take the milk and apples. The gulf between the ideals of the revolution (what the pigs pretend they are doing) and the reality of their actions gradually widens.

The role of education is an important one in the book. As they can read well, the pigs are able to dominate the animals. You should show how they use that skill to acquire knowledge – one factor in their ability to achieve and hold on to power:

- Snowball is able to prepare for Jones's attack as he has read a book of Caesar's campaigns.
- He is full of ideas for 'innovations and improvements' (Ch. 5, p. 30) for the farm that he has learnt from reading *Farmer and Stockbreeder*.
- His plans for the windmill have also come from some of Mr Jones's books, including *Electricity for Beginners*.

Contrast this with the other uses we see reading being put to in the story:

- Mr Jones falls asleep with the *News of the World* over his face. (The *News of the World* was a British tabloid newspaper with a reputation for using salacious scandals and crime stories to increase its sales.)
- Muriel simply reads 'from scraps of newspaper which she found on the rubbish heap' (Ch. 3, p. 20).
- Mollie 'refused to learn any but the six letters which spelt her own name' (Ch. 3, p. 20).

REVISION FOCUS: WHAT IS THE POINT OF EDUCATION?

Through the characters of Snowball and Napoleon, Orwell presents two contrasting views of education:

- Snowball wants to educate all the animals but to some extent his attempts are doomed.
- Napoleon concentrates his efforts on a small group, with more success.

Can you find more examples of how the characters differ in their views of education?

THEME TRACKER A02

Education and learning

- Ch. 3, pp. 20–21: The animals learn to read.
- Ch. 5, p. 30: Snowball has ideas for 'innovations and improvements' for the farm.
- Ch. 7, p. 55: The animals sing Beasts of England as a 'substitute for words [they can't] find'.

KEY CONTEXT A03

Orwell wrote (in a letter to a friend) that the failure by the animals to think for themselves was one of the morals of the story: 'I meant the moral to be that revolutions only effect a radical improvement when the masses are alert and know how to chuck out their leaders as soon as the latter have done their job.'

LANGUAGE AND POWER

THEME TRACKER (A02)

Language and power

- Ch. 3, p. 22: Squealer justifies the theft of the milk and apples.
- Ch. 5, p. 35: Squealer defends Napoleon's decision to end the debates.
- Ch. 10, p. 81: Squealer explains the pigs' work.

Language use was an important issue to Orwell. He believed that language was often used to manipulate the truth and that the thoughtless use of language made it easier to present outrageous ideas in such a way that they seem acceptable: 'Political language … is designed to make lies sound truthful and murder respectable, and to give an appearance of solidity to pure wind.'

- Orwell also wrote about 'the consciously dishonest' use of language. Look at how the use of the word 'equal' changes throughout the book: the slogan 'ALL ANIMALS ARE EQUAL BUT SOME ANIMALS ARE MORE EQUAL THAN OTHERS' (Ch. 10, p. 85) is nonsense. The word 'equal' loses its meaning here.

- The pigs can exploit the other animals as they are intelligent enough to manipulate the truth to make their evil actions seem perfectly acceptable. This is achieved through their skilful use of language. Look at how the Sixth Commandment is changed in Chapter 8.

- Even though the animals are starving, when Squealer tells them that 'they had more oats, more hay, more turnips than they had had in Jones's day' they 'believed every word of it' (Ch. 9, p. 70).

- Look at how the pigs create their own version of the truth, changing Snowball's actions at the Battle of the Cowshed.

- Look also at the **Propaganda** theme below for a more detailed explanation of the techniques used.

KEY CONTEXT (A03)

In Orwell's novel *Nineteen Eighty-Four* we are told that a character called Syme is working on a dictionary that removes words from the language. This reduces people's ability to think and to protest.

AIMING HIGH: POLITICAL LANGUAGE ⭐

In 'Politics and the English Language' Orwell wrote: 'Political language has to consist largely of euphemism … Defenceless villages are bombarded from the air, the inhabitants driven out into the countryside, the cattle machine-gunned … this is called *pacification*.' When writing about Squealer's use of language, remember to note any such euphemisms, such as the 'readjustment' (Ch. 9, p. 70) of rations, and explain the effect on the animals and how this manipulation of language stops the animals from seeing the reality of their situation.

PROPAGANDA

THEME TRACKER (A02)

Propaganda

- Ch. 8, p. 57: Squealer reads out invented statistics that the animals cannot understand.
- Ch. 7, p. 50: Squealer refers to written evidence that the animals cannot read.
- Ch. 3, p. 22: Squealer explains that milk is good for the pigs. (It is also good for other animals.)

Propaganda is a particular form of language that consciously sets out to manipulate people by presenting information in a selective way, lying by omission or creating an emotional response to what is said. The pigs in *Animal Farm* control the animals mainly through their clever use of propaganda. Orwell believed that controlling language allowed propagandists to control thought: it's no accident that Squealer is described as being able to 'turn black into white' (Ch. 2, p. 9).

REVISION FOCUS: SIMPLIFYING LANGUAGE 🕐

Look carefully at the times when slogans are used in the story. Write down which animals use these slogans and how their use of them differs. Make a note of the effect these slogans have on the other animals.

CONTEXTS

GEORGE ORWELL

George Orwell was the pseudonym of Eric Arthur Blair, who was born in Bengal, India on 25 June 1903.

- Orwell was a life-long socialist whose political beliefs led him to fight for the Republicans against Franco's fascists in the Spanish Civil War (1936–39). When the Second World War broke out, ill health prevented him from signing up to fight for Britain.
- In 1947 Orwell moved to the Scottish Hebridean island of Jura. He died of tuberculosis in 1950.

George Orwell

ORWELL'S LIFE AND *ANIMAL FARM*

Orwell's experiences in the Spanish Civil War are relevant to *Animal Farm*.

- Orwell became disillusioned with revolutionary politics after seeing the in-fighting between people who were meant to be on the same side.
- Orwell wasn't just making a point about events in post-revolutionary Russia in *Animal Farm*. He stated that the book was an attack on the way in which all dictators seize and hold on to power.
- Between 1941 and 1943, Orwell worked as an Intelligence Officer for the BBC Eastern Service, writing propaganda broadcasts for India. He also wrote several essays on the relationship between language and thought.
- Orwell was not against revolutions but he did want to show people what happens when those who lead the revolution are allowed to do as they please.

KARL MARX AND COMMUNISM

Orwell wrote that Major's speech was intended to show 'Marx's theory from the animals' point of view'. The German philosopher Karl Marx believed that in a capitalist society workers were exploited by the people they worked for, in the same way that Major claims man exploits the animals.

- Marx explained that capitalists pay workers a wage to produce goods that are then sold at a higher price than they cost to make. The capitalists then keep the profit that is made and can increase their profit by paying lower wages.
- For this reason, the capitalists and the workers would never see eye to eye, or have each other's best interests at heart. According to Marx, this situation creates a class struggle.
- Marx said that eventually the workers would rebel against the capitalists and overthrow them. They would then establish a more equal society.
- Marx wrote *Das Kapital*, which stated that society should be free and equal, and the *Communist Manifesto*, which called for workers to unite. Lenin adapted Marx's ideas to form his own brand of Communism.
- By basing Major's speech on Marx's ideas, Orwell shows us that his ideal society is a socialist one. Major's ideals are the yardstick by which we judge the pigs' new society.

KEY CONTEXT (A03)

Orwell's *The Road to Wigan Pier* (1937) drew attention to the terrible working conditions and poverty in the north of England in the 1930s and *Down and Out in Paris and London* (1933) details Orwell's experiences of life with the homeless. The welfare of ordinary people was a constant concern of Orwell's and not restricted to *Animal Farm*.

TOP TIP (A03)

Go through Major's speech and make a detailed note of any parallels with the Marxist ideas outlined here under **Karl Marx** and **Communism**.

AN ALLEGORY OF RUSSIAN HISTORY

Animal Farm is a political **allegory**. All of the events and characters represent events and figures in Russian history: the first thirty years of the Soviet Union. Orwell wrote to a friend that he intended the book to be 'a **satire** on the Russian revolution'.

- In his 1947 introduction to the Ukrainian edition of *Animal Farm*, Orwell wrote that 'it was of the utmost importance that people in Western Europe should see the Soviet regime for what it really was'. His purpose in writing the book was 'the destruction of the Soviet myth' – to teach his readers a political lesson.

- The parallels between events in *Animal Farm* and Russian history are a vital part of this purpose: to persuade us, by using a thinly veiled reference to the Soviet government, that Stalin's rule was evil and oppressive – and to show us, through the ideals he sets out in Major's speech, what an ideal **socialist** government could look like.

KEY CONTEXT (A03)

Animal Farm was written at a time when Russia was seen as an important British ally, which is one reason why Orwell found it so hard to get the story published. His depiction of Russia's leaders as pigs was seen as especially offensive.

HISTORICAL EVENTS

One of the book's greatest achievements is the way that Orwell manages to rearrange complex events from Soviet history to fit his plot. The events are not always ordered chronologically (that is, not always in the order that they happened) and some historical details are changed:

- Unlike Major, Lenin did live to lead his revolution – he became the Soviet state's first leader.

- Lenin created the Cheka, the repressive secret police. However, in *Animal Farm*, it is Napoleon (i.e. Stalin) who takes the puppies away to train them.

- The power struggle between Stalin and Trotsky happened after Lenin's death in 1924, but in *Animal Farm*, the struggle between Napoleon (i.e. Stalin) and Snowball takes place after the revolution.

- Trotsky was murdered in exile, on Stalin's orders but in *Animal Farm*, although Snowball is exiled, as far as the reader is aware he remains alive.

- The sequencing of events was carefully considered by Orwell. In March 1945 he asked for the line 'all the animals including Napoleon flung themselves to the ground' to be changed to 'all the animals except Napoleon' as it 'would be fair to Joseph Stalin, as he did stay in Moscow during the German advance'.

TOP TIP (A02)

When writing about the allegorical nature of the book, *always* remember to firmly link this to Orwell's purpose. Explain the techniques he uses to ensure that his readers understand the political message of the book, e.g. how Major's speech simplifies Marxist theory for the reader.

REVISION FOCUS: KEY STUCTURE

Orwell wrote that although 'various episodes' in *Animal Farm* are taken from the 'actual history of the Russian Revolution', the order has been changed because it was 'necessary for the symmetry of the story'. Look at the following two pages and study the changes that Orwell made to the sequencing of events. Make a note of exactly what has been altered.

- What effect do these changes have on the book?
- How does changing the order of the events help Orwell to get his political points across to the reader?

DIRECT PARALLELS

Certain real historical events correspond directly to events in *Animal Farm*, although the order of events does not exactly mirror Soviet history. The following are the main points of comparison:

Events in the Soviet Union	Events in *Animal Farm*
The Communist Party (under the leadership of Lenin) rose and took power, seizing control of the empire and executing the Romanovs (the Tsar's family).	Under the leadership of Major, the animals revolt against Jones and drive him and Mrs Jones from Manor Farm.
Communism explains life in economic and social terms. It is based on Marx's belief that the rich capitalist class exploited the proletariat and that this situation could only be reversed by revolution.	Animalism is based on Major's beliefs: 'Man is the only creature that consumes without producing ... he gives back to [the animals] the bare minimum that will prevent them from starving, and the rest he keeps for himself' (Ch. 1, p. 4).
After the revolution, Trotsky and Lenin established a Communist society in the Soviet Union (as it was then called). All property, wealth and work was meant to be divided equally between all individuals.	The pigs try to create Major's ideal society and change the farm's name from Manor Farm to Animal Farm to reflect this new beginning.
Forces loyal to the Tsar, helped by countries who saw Communism as a threat to their own power, invaded Russia. Trotsky's brilliant command of the Red Army during the Russian Civil War meant that the Bolsheviks stayed in power.	Jones and his men attempt to recapture the farm in the Battle of the Cowshed. Snowball's clever tactics mean that the animals win.
After Lenin's death, a struggle for power took place between Trotsky and Stalin. Trotsky, although favoured by Lenin, was out-manoeuvred by Stalin who then tried to eliminate all trace of him. Trotsky was forced to flee the Soviet Union. Trotsky was later airbrushed out of photographs.	Napoleon and Snowball disagree on virtually every issue. After a meeting in the barn to discuss the windmill, Napoleon drives Snowball from the farm. The animals are later told that Snowball is an enemy. Napoleon claims Snowball's idea for the windmill is his own and the history of the Battle of the Cowshed is completely rewritten.
Stalin insisted that all farms should be collectivised (come under state control). These large collective farms had to give their produce to the government, something that was violently opposed by the farmers. He also tried to modernise Soviet industry through his Five-Year Plans – the success of which he then exaggerated.	Napoleon instructs the hens to sell their eggs, but they smash them rather then let him sell them. The animals work hard to build a windmill on the farm.
The Soviet Union endured several famines as the result of Stalin's economic policies. It is thought that at least 5 million people starved to death between 1932 and 1934. Some historians think that Stalin deliberately starved some areas of Russia (for example, Ukraine) to eliminate opposition.	Napoleon shows Whymper the apparently full grain stores (which are mainly filled with sand). The animals suffer increasingly from hunger after Napoleon comes to power, while the pigs are well fed.

Events in the Soviet Union	Events in *Animal Farm*
Stalin had complete control over the Soviet Union. He created a cult of personality around himself: Russians were told that he was the wisest man in the world. Pictures of him were displayed in schools and factories. He used propaganda to convince the Russian people that only he could protect them.	Napoleon uses a combination of terror and propaganda to become a dictator. Squealer is crucial in convincing the animals that Napoleon has only their best interests at heart. A portrait of Napoleon is painted on the barn wall. Songs, poems and speeches praising life on the farm are written.
Stalin's rival Kirov was murdered in 1934 (some historians think on Stalin's orders) and this event was used by Stalin as a pretext for the ruthless elimination of any sources of potential opposition during the Purges of the 1930s. Between 1934 and 1938, 7 million people disappeared, many of them ordinary Russians. Most were executed or sent to gulags (slave labour camps). The most important victims were given 'show trials' and made to confess publicly to non-existent crimes (often to save their families from punishment) before they were executed.	Napoleon eliminates Snowball, who is his rival for leadership of the farm, to ensure that his position is unchallenged. Napoleon gets rid of the four porkers who protested against the abolition of the Sunday debates and the hens who led the egg rebellion by accusing them of working in league with Snowball to destroy the farm. He stages a show trial, where the animals confess publicly to their supposed crimes before being slaughtered.
In an effort to protect the Soviet Union from attack, Stalin negotiated with both Britain and Hitler's Germany. His treaty with Germany was seen as worthless when Germany invaded the Soviet Union in 1941. The Germans were later defeated at the Battle of Stalingrad, but not before Russia suffered heavy casualties.	Napoleon has dealings with both Frederick and Pilkington over selling the timber and is finally tricked by Frederick who pays in forged notes. The animals defeat Frederick's men in the Battle of the Windmill but it is a hard and painful struggle.
At the Tehran Conference in 1943, the Soviet Union, Britain and the United States of America claimed to be allies. A few years later, the Cold War began, which placed the Soviet Union against its wartime allies.	The pigs and farmers have dinner together but their friendship is destroyed when both sides are discovered to have cheated at cards.

SETTINGS

The book is set on a farm, an unlikely setting for a revolution.

- Orwell paints a fairly realistic picture of farm life: the feeding, watering and milking of the animals are all described.
- The farm animals are anthropomorphic, although they still behave in ways characteristic of their species.
- The simple setting makes the book's political ideas easier to understand, so that the book's themes can reach its widest audience.

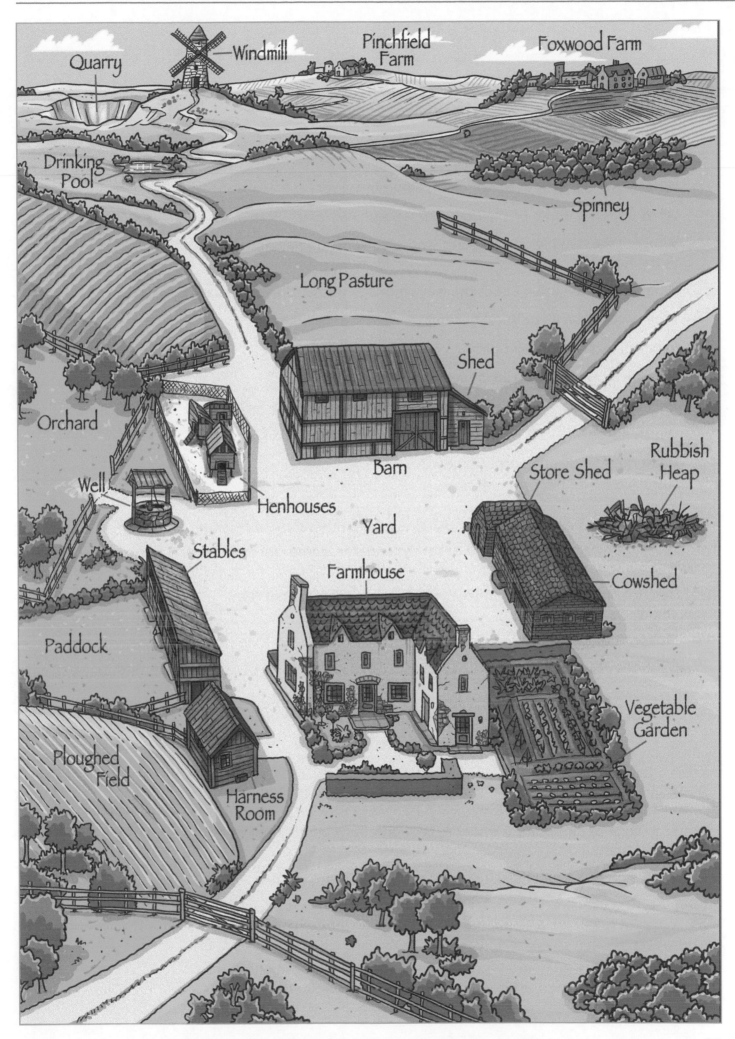

PROGRESS AND REVISION CHECK

SECTION ONE: CHECK YOUR KNOWLEDGE

Answer these quick questions to test your basic knowledge of the themes, contexts and settings of the text:

1 Whose rise to power does Napoleon's journey mirror?

2 What does the Battle of the Cowshed represent?

3 Who are the two historical figures whose power struggle is mirrored in the book?

4 What did Orwell think about the way language was used by politicians?

5 What were Orwell's political beliefs?

6 In which war did Orwell fight?

7 For which organisation did Orwell write propaganda?

8 How did Karl Marx describe the way in which a capitalist society works?

9 Which historical event is mirrored in the Battle of the Windmill?

10 What does 'anthropomorphic' mean?

SECTION TWO: CHECK YOUR UNDERSTANDING

This task requires more thought and a slightly longer response. Try to write at least three to four paragraphs.

Task: Describe the steps Napoleon takes to seize power on Animal Farm. Think about:

- How he gains support
- How he keeps hold of power

PROGRESS CHECK

GOOD PROGRESS

I can:

- explain the main themes, contexts and settings in the text and how they contribute to the effect on the reader. ☐
- use a range of appropriate evidence to support any points I make about these elements. ☐

EXCELLENT PROGRESS

I can:

- analyse in detail the way themes are developed and presented across the text. ☐
- refer closely to key aspects of context and setting and the implications they have for the writer's viewpoint, and the interpretation of relationships and ideas. ☐

FORM

OVERVIEW

- Orwell himself wrote that *Animal Farm* was primarily 'a satire on the Russian revolution'. *Animal Farm* is also an allegory of events in Russian history (see **An allegory of Russian history** in **Part Four: Contexts**).

- Orwell makes use of the beast fable form (stories in which animal characters are used to make serious moral points) for a particular reason. *Animal Farm* is an explicitly moral book, of which Orwell wrote: 'I meant the moral to be that revolutions only effect a radical improvement when the masses are alert and know how to chuck out their leaders as soon as the latter have done their job.'

- *Animal Farm* is subtitled 'A Fairy Story', drawing our attention to the supposedly fictitious events in the story. Its simple language and anthropomorphic characters are in keeping with this form.

SATIRE

What is satire?	A satire is a written attack that makes something look foolish or unpleasant. Ironic humour is often used to draw our attention to what the author is attacking.
Example	Minimus's poem *'Friend of the fatherless!'* (Ch. 8, p. 58)
Effect	The poem is unintentionally humorous as we can see the gap between his description of the farm and the reality of life under Napoleon.

Animal Farm is a satire on political power. Orwell uses the following techniques in his satire:

- Animal stereotypes: his choice of animal to represent different historical figures or ideas is satirical. He uses mainly negative representations, for example, the sheep (traditionally regarded as stupid animals) are used to represent the public as an unthinking 'mob'. The satire is effective as Orwell expects us to be aware of how the characters should behave.

- Political allegory: the symbols used are obvious – as you would expect in an allegory. The farm represents Russia; Napoleon represents Stalin. World events are reduced to the level of a farmyard. The satire also makes complex political events, such as the German invasion of Russia (shown here as the Battle of the Windmill), easy for us to understand.

- Ridicule: by reducing well-known political figures to the level of farmyard animals (and unflattering ones at that), Orwell trivialises and ridicules his targets. For example, Napoleon's black cockerel and the poems composed in his honour are seen as ludicrous, contrary to the effect of grandeur and power for which Napoleon strives.

Satire uses mockery to criticise the object of its scorn. It has a moral purpose. By criticising Napoleon's regime, Orwell expects us to share his view of what society *should* be like: equal, just and free.

TOP TIP (A02)

When writing about *Animal Farm* as a satire, be sure to explain in detail how this satirical effect is created. It's important that you not only identify the techniques he uses but also intelligently explain the *effect* that they have on the reader.

AIMING HIGH: *ANIMAL FARM* AS A FAIRY STORY ⭐

Part of the reason for the continued popularity of *Animal Farm* is its apparent simplicity. The book is set in a farmyard, its storyline progresses in clear stages, its main characters are animals: it seems at first to be a perfect children's book.

- It's useful to note how the simplicity of the book and its omniscient narrator support its subtitle 'A Fairy Story'.

- This is also reinforced by words such as 'hen-houses', 'pop-holes' (Ch. 1, p. 1) which give us a strong sense of the story's farmyard setting – strengthening the sense of a traditional fairy story, such as 'Chicken Licken'.

- Animals are also introduced to us in a list-like way as they come into the barn, mirroring the way characters are often introduced in fairy tales (for example, 'Goldilocks').

- You should explain how the simple storyline; straightforward, sometimes comic, characters and seemingly naïve tone stop *Animal Farm* from being seen as a dry political pamphlet and allow Orwell's message to reach the widest possible audience in a readable form.

- You should also point out that Orwell subverts the genre he is writing in. We expect fairy tales to be about the battle between good and evil – as in *Animal Farm* – but in this book, good is seen to be punished rather than rewarded.

- The ending's ambiguity leaves us thinking the worst – that there is no possible happy ending to the story. We don't expect fairy tales to be nightmares. We conclude that *Animal Farm* is not a fairy story at all, but a bleak political satire.

TOP TIP (A02)

Think about how the events in the farmhouse at the end of Chapter 10 would come across if they were seen from Napoleon's or Benjamin's point of view. What effect would losing an omniscient view of events have on our understanding of this final scene?

BEAST FABLE

What is a beast fable?	A beast fable is a story in which animal characters are used to make serious moral points.
Example	'Benjamin could read as well as any pig, but never exercised his faculty.' (Ch. 3, p. 20)
Effect	Orwell shows us what happens if people are apathetic about their leaders.

In beast fables, such as *Aesop's Fables*, characters do not behave in a realistic way but are symbolic of certain attitudes. Animals are often the main characters in children's books (such as *The Wind in the Willows* or *The Jungle Book*) for a similar reason. They do not have to be as 'realistic' as characters in other books and can be given one single, overriding personality trait.

Unlike most beast fables, though, the ending of *Animal Farm* is ambiguous. There is no clear sense of how life will turn out for the animals. No clear moral is stated at the end of the story, although Orwell's message throughout the text is clear.

STRUCTURE

OVERVIEW

- In keeping with the book's subtitle, *Animal Farm* has a simple structure.
- The book's plot is circular. This highlights the broken promises and failed hopes of the animals' rebellion.
- As befits an allegory, the events in *Animal Farm* mirror historical events: those of the Russian Revolution and the history of the Soviet Union under Stalin. However, these events are not shown chronologically. Orwell reorders them to suit his narrative.
- The Seven Commandments are used by Orwell to chart the pigs' transformation into mankind. (Remember that, according to Major, 'Man is the only real enemy we have' (Ch.1, p. 4).)
- Orwell creates events that appear to mirror each other: the Battles of the Cowshed and Windmill, the destruction of the windmill and the deaths of animals that oppose Napoleon. The juxtaposition of these events in the story is used to emphasise the farm's descent into tyranny.

TOP TIP (A02)

When writing about the structure of the story, think about the ways in which Orwell uses repetition to make a satiric point. How is the Battle of the Cowshed echoed throughout the story, for example?

A CIRCULAR PLOT?

The **novella** is divided into ten chapters and could be said to have a circular plot in that the animals at the end are in a similar position to where they started.

- The book charts the corruption of Major's principles in stages. Chapter 1 sets out the rebellion's high ideals and acts as a marker by which we judge the pigs' subsequent actions.
- The turning point comes once Napoleon orders the execution of the pigs and the hens. Then there is a speedy descent into further betrayal and tyranny.
- Life on the farm deteriorates quickly once the murders take place – and it is not long before the pigs are walking on their hind legs, installing a phone and dressing in human clothing.
- By end of the book, Napoleon sleeps in Jones's bed, uses his crockery and drinks alcohol.
- The circular nature of the plot is used by Orwell to highlight the depth of Napoleon's descent and the irony of the revolution.
- However, the situation is worse than at the start of the book, as the pigs have betrayed the animals' trust.

TOP TIP: WRITING ABOUT THE SEVEN COMMANDMENTS (A02)

It's useful to show how Orwell charts the farm's decline into tyranny by the gradual violation of each of the Seven Commandments. List the rules that are agreed by all the animals at the outset of the story and then select an example to show how each Commandment is broken. Which of the violations is the most serious? Why?

LANGUAGE

OVERVIEW

- Orwell frequently wrote about language and its importance.
- In his essay 'Why I Write', Orwell commented that good writing was 'like a windowpane' – a good description of the plain language in which the majority of *Animal Farm* is written.
- While the language of the book seems almost naïve at times, its apparent simplicity amplifies the book's irony.
- Orwell was concerned about the power of language and the way it could be used to manipulate people's thoughts and beliefs (see **Language and power** in **Part Four: Themes**).

LANGUAGE DEVICE: NARRATIVE VOICE

What is narrative voice?	Narrative voice is the style in which a character or the narrator (or author) addresses the reader.
Example	'Mr. Jones, of the Manor Farm, had locked the hen-houses for the night, but was too drunk to remember to shut the pop-holes.' (Ch. 1, p. 1)
Effect	The opening sentence of the book mirrors the detached language and sentence structure of a traditional storyteller, in keeping with the book's subtitle. 'A Fairy Story'.

Orwell uses a third person, omniscient narrator to tell us the story of Animal Farm. A third-person narrator is a god-like, all-knowing figure, who sees everything that happens in the story – and can even tell us what each character is thinking. Most fairy stories and fables have a narrator, who acts as a story-teller. However, there are also other reasons why Orwell uses this technique:

- The novella is written in the sort of simple language we would expect to find in a fairy tale. Phrases like 'As soon as the light in the bedroom went out there was a stirring and a fluttering all through the farm buildings' (Ch. 1, p. 1) encourage us to think that this will be a traditional children's story.
- You need to show that although we are often told the animals' interpretation of events, Orwell is careful to use phrases that leave us in no doubt about what is really happening. For example, when Squealer is found at the bottom of the ladder in the night, it is described as 'a strange incident which hardly anyone was able to understand' (Ch. 8, p. 68). The animals do not know what has happened but we see that Squealer has been caught red-handed changing the Commandments, and has fallen off the ladder because he is drunk. The ironic gap between what the animals see happening and what we know has really happened is exploited by Orwell to make a satirical point.

TOP TIP (A02)

You need to show how Orwell repeats phrases such as 'worked like slaves' (Ch. 6, p. 37) throughout the book to remind us of the animals' constant suffering and the effect of the pigs' actions. The repetition of simple phrases is also typical of fairy tales.

AIMING HIGH: SHIFTS IN TONE

Look at how Orwell uses descriptive language in order to leave us in no doubt that the revolution is a good thing. The portrayal of the farm after the revolution is poetic ('sweet summer grass') and contains an evocative physical description of the animals' activities ('snuffled its rich scent') (Ch. 2, p. 13), unlike the usually plain language used elsewhere in the text.

Notice also that Orwell's style is so seemingly 'transparent' and simple that it is sometimes easy to forget that our views of the story's events and characters are being carefully directed.

KEY CONTEXT   A03

Orwell wrote in his essay 'Why I Write': '*Animal Farm* was the first book in which I tried, with full consciousness of what I was doing, to fuse political purpose and artistic purpose into one whole.' Do you think he succeeded?

TOP TIP: WRITING ABOUT THE PIGS' VOICE   A02

Animal Farm is written in a plain, simple language. You could point out how this contrasts with the elitist language used by the pigs. Major's authoritative use of imperatives – 'You cows', 'And you hens' (Ch. 1, p. 4) – adds authority. Snowball uses Jargon to suggest that a wing should not be counted as a leg, as it is 'an organ of propulsion and not of manipulation' (Ch. 3, p. 21). Jargon makes the speaker sound clever and the technique is also used by Squealer to hide his real meanings and motives.

Note how the pigs speak in an entirely different register to that used by the other animals. Their different style of language sets them apart and allows them to confuse and control the other animals on the farm.

EXAM FOCUS: SQUEALER'S TECHNIQUES   A02

Technique	Example
Rhetorical questions	The animals are repeatedly asked if they want Jones back, 'Do you know what would happen if we pigs failed in our duty? Jones would come back!' (Ch. 3, p. 22). In this case, there is also an implicit threat that if they refuse to do as the pigs say, this will happen.
Statistics	Squealer 'would read out to them lists of figures' (Ch. 8, p. 57). He creates an illusion of life on the farm that the animals are incapable of questioning.
Subversion	The pigs completely change the meaning of words. They use the word 'equality' to mean its opposite. It is logically impossible for anyone to be 'more equal' than another.
Obfuscation	The pigs mislead the animals by deliberately using words that the other animals don't understand: 'Squealer told them that the pigs had to expend enormous labours every day upon mysterious things called "files", "reports", "minutes" and "memoranda"' (Ch. 10, p. 81).

LANGUAGE DEVICE: IRONY

What is irony?	Irony is using words to express something different from, and often opposite to, their literal meaning.
Example	'once a week there should be held something called a Spontaneous Demonstration, the object of which was to celebrate the struggles and triumphs of Animal Farm.' (Ch. 9, p. 72)
Effect	Something spontaneous cannot be planned. The ironic gap between the name of the demonstration and the reality of the animals' lives shows us how the pigs create the impression that life on the farm is positive.

- We are told that the animals have 'hardships' to face but that they have 'a greater dignity' in their lives as there are 'more songs, more speeches, more processions' (Ch. 9, p. 72). The reader can see that the pigs are distracting the animals from the harsh reality of their lives.

- The animals' pride that their work is 'for the benefit of themselves' and not for 'a pack of idle, thieving human beings' (Ch. 6, p. 37) is undercut by the reader's awareness that the animals are being exploited in exactly this way by the pigs.

LANGUAGE DEVICE: SYMBOLISM

What is symbolism?	Symbolism is using an object or person to represent something else.
Example	'The flag was green, Snowball explained, to represent the green fields of England, while the hoof and horn signified the future Republic of the Animals' (Ch. 3, p. 18). Within the story's allegory, the hoof and horn are a reference to the hammer and sickle of the Soviet flag.
Effect	Reducing the symbol of a powerful ally (as Soviet Russia was when Orwell wrote this book) to Snowball's flag ridicules the Soviet state.

Animal Farm is a political allegory, so we would expect Orwell to make use of symbols to represent certain events and ideas in Soviet history:

- Characters are used symbolically. Snowball and Napoleon represent Trotsky and Stalin and their bitter struggle for power.
- The windmill represents Stalin's industrialisation of Russia and the sacrifices made by the Russian people under his Five-Year Plans.
- The Battle of the Windmill represents the Battle of Stalingrad, at which Soviet forces defeated Hitler's invading German army – but at huge cost to themselves.
- Some of these symbols are satirical. Orwell mocks Stalin by reducing him to a 'fierce-looking' (Ch. 2, p. 9) boar (one of the reasons why Orwell had difficulty getting the book published).

TOP TIP (A01)

Don't forget to comment on the symbolism of some of the characters' names. Why does Moses's name suit him?

PROGRESS AND REVISION CHECK

SECTION ONE: CHECK YOUR KNOWLEDGE

Answer these quick questions to test your basic knowledge of the form, structure and language of the text:

1. What is the book's subtitle?

2. Who tells us the story of *Animal Farm*?

3. What is satire?

4. How is the description that the animals 'worked like slaves' (Ch. 6, p. 37) ironic?

5. What symbol does Orwell use at the end of the book to show us that the pigs have become as vicious as Mr Jones?

6. What is a fable?

7. What is a stereotype?

8. What list of rules is used by Orwell to mark how the pigs transform into humans?

9. What is the windmill a symbol of?

10. What is jargon?

SECTION TWO: CHECK YOUR UNDERSTANDING

This task requires more thought and a slightly longer response. Try to write at least three to four paragraphs.

Task: *Animal Farm* is subtitled 'A Fairy Story'. How accurately does this describe the book? Think about:

- What we expect to find in a fairy story
- What we find in *Animal Farm*

PROGRESS CHECK

GOOD PROGRESS

I can:

- explain how Orwell uses form, structure and language to develop the action, show relationships and develop ideas. ☐
- use relevant quotations to support the points I make, and refer to the effect of some language choices. ☐

EXCELLENT PROGRESS

I can:

- analyse in detail Orwell's use of particular forms, structures and language techniques to convey ideas, create characters and evoke mood or setting. ☐
- select from a range of evidence, including apt quotations, to infer the effect of particular language choices, and to develop wider interpretations. ☐

UNDERSTANDING THE QUESTION

For your exam, you will be answering a question on the whole text and/or a question on an extract from *Animal Farm*. Check with your teacher to see what sort of question you are doing. Whatever the task, questions in exams will need **decoding**. This means highlighting and understanding the key words so that the answer you write is relevant.

BREAK DOWN THE QUESTION

Pick out the **key words** or phrases. For example:

Question: How does George Orwell **present the significance of Major's speech** in *Animal Farm*? Write about:

- What Major says in his speech
- How Orwell uses the speech to express his idea of an ideal society

What does this tell you?

- Focus on **Major** but also on **why** what he says is **significant**.
- The word **'present'** tells you that you should focus on the way Orwell reveals the ideas in Major's speech, i.e. the techniques he uses.

PLANNING YOUR ANSWER

It is vital that you generate ideas quickly, and plan your answer efficiently when you sit the exam. Stick to your plan and, with a watch at your side, tick off each part as you progress.

STAGE 1: GENERATE IDEAS QUICKLY

Very briefly **list your key ideas** based on the question you have **decoded**. For example:

- *Who Major represents*
- *What Major tells the animals*
- *Examples in the text of an ideal society*

STAGE 2: JOT DOWN USEFUL QUOTATIONS (OR KEY EVENTS)

For example:

- *Major warns the animals about the possible dangers of fighting mankind*
- *Major: 'Remember also that in fighting against Man, we must not come to resemble him' (Chapter 1)*

STAGE 3: PLAN FOR PARAGRAPHS

Use paragraphs to plan your answer. For example:

Paragraph	Point
Paragraph 1:	**Introduce** the **argument** you wish to make: *'Animal Farm' is a satire written by Orwell to demonstrate how a society can descend into dictatorship. Major's speech is vital because Orwell uses it to establish the fundamental principles of a fair and just society at the start of the story.*
Paragraph 2:	Your first point: *Orwell makes clear to us that Major's words are important – he emphasises how much the animals respect him, so that we also accept that what Major says is true. In this way, Major's speech lays the moral foundations for the rest of the story.*
Paragraph 3:	Your second point: *Major's speech is important because it sets out in detail how the animals are exploited by man. Major's use of imperatives (for example, 'No animal in England is free') leaves no room to doubt the validity of his argument and he inspires the animals to rebellion.*
Paragraph 4:	Your third point: *Major's speech is vital because it provides the yardstick by which we judge the pigs' actions in the rest of the book. When Boxer meets the fate that Major predicted and the pigs mirror 'the habits of Man', we recognise that the pigs have become 'evil'.*
Paragraph 5:	Your fourth point: *'Animal Farm' is a political allegory, which Orwell wrote to criticise the Soviet government. Major's speech is a key element of this because it summarises Marxist philosophy, while we see Napoleon – or Stalin – move away from these ideals towards tyranny.*
(You may want to add further paragraphs if you have time.)	
Conclusion:	**Sum up** your argument: *Orwell presents his political ideas in the simplified allegorical form of Major's speech so that his readers understand that Soviet Russia was not the ideal – socialist – society set out by Marx but a tyranny run by a ruthless dictator.*

TOP TIP (A02)

When discussing Orwell's language, make sure you refer to the techniques he uses, and, most importantly, the *effect* of those techniques. Don't just write, *Orwell uses lots of rhetorical questions here*, write, *Orwell's use of rhetorical questions shows/ demonstrates/ conveys the ideas that ....*

RESPONDING TO WRITERS' EFFECTS

The two most important assessment objectives are **AO1** and **AO2**. They are about *what* writers do (the choices they make, and the effects these create), *what* your ideas are (your analysis and interpretation), and *how* you write about them (how well you explain your ideas).

ASSESSMENT OBJECTIVE 1

What does it say?	What does it mean?	Dos and don'ts
Read, understand and respond to texts. Students should be able to: ● Maintain a critical style and develop an informed personal response ● Use textual references, including quotations, to support and illustrate interpretations	You must: ● Use some of the literary terms you have learned (correctly!) ● Write in a professional way (not a sloppy, chatty way) ● Show you have thought for yourself ● Back up your ideas with examples, including quotations	**Don't write:** *Clover is a really nice character. Orwell uses lots of nice words to describe her. 'Clover was a stout, motherly mare.'* **Do write:** *Orwell presents Clover throughout the text as a caring and decent character, for example when she 'makes a sort of wall' with her hoof to protect the ducklings in Chapter 1.*

IMPROVING YOUR CRITICAL STYLE

Use a variety of words and phrases to show effects. For example:

Orwell *suggests ..., conveys ..., implies ..., explores ..., demonstrates ..., signals ..., describes how ..., shows how ...*

I/we *(as readers) infer ..., recognise ..., understand ..., question ...*

For example, look at these two alternative paragraphs by different students about Napoleon. Note the difference in the quality of expression.

Student A:

> This sounds as if George Orwell is speaking

> It could 'mean' this, but there are other possibilities

Orwell says that Napoleon is really horrible to Snowball in Chapter 5. He walked into Snowball's shed and urinated over the plans'. This means that Napoleon is being cruel. This means that he doesn't care if Snowball knows he doesn't like them. Orwell is saying Napoleon and Snowball are at war with each other.

> Very chatty and informal

> Better to use other words or phrases than 'say' or 'saying'

Student B:

Clear and precise language	Orwell presents Napoleon in an unpleasant light when he sees Snowball's plans for the windmill in Chapter 5. He demonstrates his contempt for Snowball's scheme by walking out 'without uttering a word' implying that he is also trying to intimidate Snowball. Orwell also seems to be saying that Napoleon will use actions rather than words to show his opposition.

Good variety of vocabulary

This helps introduce an interpretation – rather than saying 'this is what it means'

Using 'seems' allows the student to explore the idea rather than state it bluntly as fact

ASSESSMENT OBJECTIVE 2

What does it say?	What does it mean?	Dos and don'ts
Analyse the language, form and structure used by the writer to create meanings and effects, using relevant subject terminology where appropriate.	'Analyse' – comment **in detail** on **particular aspects** of the text or language 'Language' – vocabulary, imagery, variety of sentences, dialogue/speech, etc. 'Form' – **how** the story is told (e.g. first person narrative, letters, diaries, chapters) 'Structure' – the **order** in which events are revealed, or in which characters appear, or descriptions are presented 'create meanings' – what can we, as readers, **infer** from what the writer tells us? What is **implied**? 'Subject terminology' – **words** you should use when **writing** about plays, such as 'character', 'protagonist', 'imagery', etc.	**Don't write:** *The writing is really descriptive in this bit so I get a good picture of what the farm looks like.* **Do write:** *Orwell **emphasises** the beauty of the farm through Clover's view of it after the executions: 'the bursting hedges were gilded by the level rays of the sun'. The change in pace and **use** of the words 'bursting' and 'gilded' create a **lyrical**, **pastoral** image that **heightens** the **tragedy**.*

THE THREE 'I'S

- Firstly, the best analysis focuses on specific ideas, events or uses of language and thinks about what is **implied**.
- This means drawing **inferences**. After Boxer's death in Chapter 9, it is stated 'that from somewhere or other' the pigs 'had acquired the money to buy themselves another case of whisky'. The phrase 'somewhere or other' is ironic, suggesting that the animals cannot see what the reader can: that the pigs have sold Boxer to the knacker and spent the money on alcohol.
- From the inferences you make across the text as a whole, you can arrive at your own **interpretation** – a sense of the bigger picture, a wider evaluation of a person, relationship or idea, for example, in this case, the manner in which the animals have had their thoughts manipulated.

USING QUOTATIONS

One of the secrets of success in writing exam essays is to use quotations **effectively**. There are five basic principles:

1. Only quote what is most useful.

2. Do not use a quotation that repeats what you have just written.

3. Put quotation marks, e.g. ' ', around the quotation.

4. Write the quotation exactly as it appears in the original.

5. Use the quotation so that it fits neatly into your sentence.

EXAM FOCUS: USING QUOTATIONS A01

Quotations should be used to develop the line of thought in your essay and 'zoom in' on key details, such as language choices. The example below shows a clear and effective way of doing this:

Gives an apt quotation

> Orwell presents Squealer as a clever speaker. He can twist words and 'turn black into white'. This suggests that Squealer can be devious.

Makes a clear point

Explains the effect of the quotation

However, really **high-level responses** will go further. They will make an even more precise point, support it with an even more appropriate quotation, focus in on particular words and phrases and explain the effect or what is implied to make a wider point or draw inferences. Here is an example:

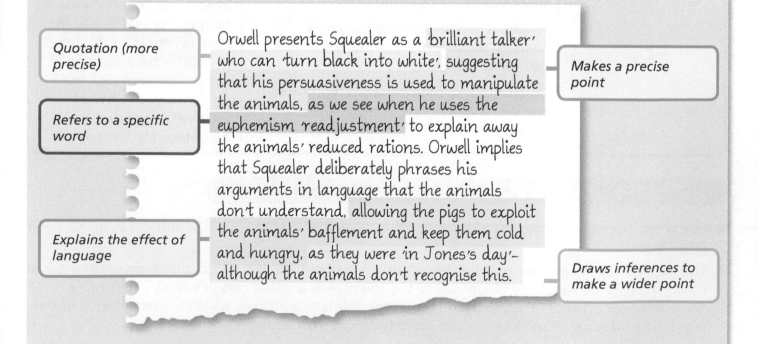

Quotation (more precise)

Refers to a specific word

Explains the effect of language

> Orwell presents Squealer as a 'brilliant talker' who can 'turn black into white', suggesting that his persuasiveness is used to manipulate the animals, as we see when he uses the euphemism 'readjustment' to explain away the animals' reduced rations. Orwell implies that Squealer deliberately phrases his arguments in language that the animals don't understand, allowing the pigs to exploit the animals' bafflement and keep them cold and hungry, as they were 'in Jones's day'— although the animals don't recognise this.

Makes a precise point

Draws inferences to make a wider point

SPELLING, PUNCTUATION AND GRAMMAR

SPELLING

Remember to spell correctly the **author's** name, the names of all the **characters** and the names of **places**.

A good idea is to list some of the key spellings you know you sometimes get wrong *before* the exam starts. Then use it to check as you go along. Sometimes it is easy to make small errors as you write but if you have your key word list nearby you can check against it.

PUNCTUATION

Remember:

- Use **full-stops and commas in sentences accurately to make clear points.** Don't write long, rambling sentences that don't make sense; equally, avoid a lot of short repetitive ones. Write in a fluent way, using linking words and phrases, and use **inverted commas** for **quotations**:

Don't write	Do write
Boxer and Benjamin are good friends they seem to behave differently. This is as the story progresses. This may be due to their different attitudes towards the pigs.	*Boxer and Benjamin are good friends **although** they seem to develop different outlooks on life on the farm as the story progresses. This may be due to their different attitudes towards the pigs.*

GRAMMAR

When you are writing about the text, make sure you:

- Use the present tense for discussing what the writer does, e.g. *Orwell **presents** Moses as deceitful and untrustworthy* NOT *Orwell **presented** Moses as deceitful and untrustworthy.*
- Use pronouns and references back to make your writing flow.

Don't write	Do write
While Mollie seems to be a more capable reader than Boxer and Clover, Mollie's use of this skill simply to write her own name made the mare appear foolish.	*While Mollie seems to be a more capable reader than Boxer and Clover, **her** use of this skill to simply write her own name **makes her** appear foolish.*

TOP TIP (A04)

Remember that spelling, punctuation and grammar are worth **approximately 5%** of your overall marks, which could mean the difference between one grade and another.

TOP TIP (A04)

Practise your spellings of key literature terms you might use when writing about the text such as: ironic, omniscient narrator, simile, metaphor, imagery, protagonist, character, theme, hierarchy, etc.

TOP TIP (A04)

Enliven your essay by varying the way your sentences begin. For example, *The animals believe Squealer's explanation, despite their misgivings,* can also be written as: *Despite their misgivings, the animals believe Squealer's explanation.*

ANNOTATED SAMPLE ANSWERS

This section provides three sample responses, one at **mid** level, one at a **good** level and one at a **very high** level.

> **Question: How does Orwell use Boxer to present ideas about power in the text?**
>
> Write about:
>
> - How Orwell presents Boxer
> - How Orwell uses Boxer to present ideas about power

SAMPLE ANSWER 1

A01 Introduces basic view of Boxer

A01 Quotation, but not fluently embedded

Orwell presents Boxer as a good character as he works very hard in the story and believes in the revolution. The way he speaks shows that he doesn't understand the ideas behind the revolution but believes in them anyway. 'Napoleon is always right' shows that he trusts the pigs and never questions what they are doing.

A01 Specific point of view

A01 Too informal; needs to have a critical style

Another thing is that he is the strongest character on the farm and without him the other animals would be stuck. For example, Orwell says, 'Boxer was the admiration of everybody' so we know we are meant to think he is basically a good person. Orwell also says 'the entire work of the farm seemed to rest upon his mighty shoulders' so he seems trustworthy and important to us. He works hard on the farm and helps to get in the harvest twice and build the windmill. He also fights to defend the farm even though the second time he does, at the Battle of the Windmill, he is badly hurt.

A01 New point clearly signalled in new paragraph

A01 A basic view of Boxer's actions in the story

Boxer is powerful in the Battle of the Cowshed. He is at the front of the fighting and is really brave and is one of the reasons that the animals win. He is really upset when he thinks he has killed the stable-lad. Snowball says that this doesn't matter and that 'the only good human being is a dead one'. This shows us that Snowball is cruel and if he ruled Animal Farm things might not be much different.

A02 Not relevant to this part of the essay, which is about Boxer

Boxer is strong and has that sort of power but is not clever. He finds it very hard to learn to read and forgets what he has learned very easily. Because this is a political book, Orwell uses him to show how Russian working people got badly treated by their government. Once Boxer loses his strength the pigs sell him off for glue so Orwell is saying that once working people can't work anymore governments don't care about them and treat them cruelly. We like Boxer so we think that this is really wrong.

To end with we see that Boxer is a strong character and so that is how he is powerful. But the pigs' power is cleverness and that means they can defeat him. So Orwell is saying that you can't win unless you are as clever as the government.

A03
Explanation is related to historical context but is clumsily expressed

A01
An attempt to sum up but a bit weakly expressed

MID LEVEL

Comment
There are some good points made here and a viewpoint comes across but the style is rather chatty and informal in places. The writer needs to refer more to Orwell himself and what *he* does, and there is little reference to language devices or techniques. There is one comment on context but it is fleeting.

For a Good Level:
- Use a more formal and critical vocabulary rather than chatty, informal words and phrases.
- Embed quotations into sentences more fluently so that they flow and are easy to follow.
- Comment in detail on the effect of language choices made by Orwell.

SAMPLE ANSWER 2

A01 Introduction sets up answer well with some sense of authorial purpose

Orwell presents Boxer as someone who is powerful and loyal. He is one of the 'good' characters in the book and that is something Orwell makes use of later in the story.

A02 Zooms in on key phrase and explains its effect

A01 Quotation fluently embedded into the sentence

From the start, we are told that Boxer is a big creature with 'vast hairy hoofs' that he sets down 'with great care lest there should be some small animal concealed in the straw.' The fact that he takes 'great care' not to hurt smaller creatures shows how considerate Boxer is. We also see this when he thinks he has killed the stable-lad. This makes us feel sympathetic towards him. He is strong but kindhearted.

A01 Paragraph introduces new point

Orwell also shows that Boxer is loyal. We can see this when Boxer is described as one of the revolution's most 'faithful disciples'. The word 'faithful' tells us that Boxer simply follows what the pigs say because he trusts them, like people follow religions. He and Clover have 'great difficulty in thinking anything out for themselves' – although he is loyal he can't think for himself and has to rely on the pigs, which Orwell shows later is a weakness.

A02 Analysis of key word and comment on text as a whole

A01 A well-developed, clear personal interpretation

Orwell also demonstrates this loyalty when Boxer is attacked by the dogs at the meeting. It seems to happen out of nowhere, as the attack is 'to the animals' amazement'. Even when the dogs strike against Boxer, he looks to Napoleon to see what to do. To the animals, the attack is a shock, they think the dogs have gone 'mad' but we know it has been planned: earlier Squealer gave Boxer an 'ugly look' when he questioned Squealer's criticism of Snowball at the Battle of the Cowshed so we know that Napoleon planned the attack to get rid of Boxer but didn't expect Boxer to be powerful enough to defeat three dogs. This threat is repeated when we see Boxer being taken away from the farm and to the knacker's. Once he is of no use to Napoleon, he gets rid of Boxer. So we see that Napoleon is ruthless and that once Boxer's physical power is gone there is nothing left to protect him.

A01 Point taken a stage further in reference to a later part of the text

One of the most upsetting parts of the book is Boxer's removal from the farm in Chapter 9. Even when he collapses, he thinks about the farm first, telling the other animals that he has left enough stone to build the rest of the windmill. So this makes what happens to him even worse – especially as the pigs sell him for enough money to buy a crate of whisky. It doesn't matter if Boxer is 'one of the most loyal workers on the farm', once he has collapsed the pigs just use him another way.

Orwell also uses Boxer to show us how powerful the working classes can be. 'Animal Farm' is an allegory and Boxer represents the working class, ordinary people. Orwell uses Boxer to show us that working people don't know their strength and that they can be easily exploited by ruthless leaders, in the same way that Orwell thought that the Russian people had been exploited by Stalin. Boxer represents workers like Alexey Stakhanov, who were praised for their very hard work.

A03

Good contextual knowledge

In conclusion, Orwell wants us to see Boxer as the hero of the story. Orwell uses the fact that we sympathise with the loyal, hardworking, caring Boxer to make us realise the suffering that the ordinary Russian working class had to endure as a result of Stalin's actions. Without Boxer, Orwell's satire would be much less effective.

GOOD LEVEL

Comment
This is a generally fluent and well-argued response, which explores the presentation of Boxer in some detail and has an awareness of authorial purpose. There is some close analysis of key words and phrases to get points across, and some evidence of personal interpretation. Expression is generally good, and quotations are fluently embedded, but the use of phases such as 'So we see' is a little too informal.

For a High Level:
- Develop ideas about the social context more fully.
- Expand the style of expression by using a wider vocabulary so more subtle ideas can be developed.
- Vary opening sentences in paragraphs so that the essay can introduce ideas in more interesting ways.

SAMPLE ANSWER 3

A01 Excellent opening sets up importance of Boxer in the action of the text and his presentation

A03 Clear sense of understanding of context in which the book is written and authorial purpose

A04 Uses a range of sentence structure for clarity and demonstrates good use of punctuation

A01 An informed response with good use of quotation

A01 Clear grasp of text, relating parts to the whole

A02 Excellent understanding of authorial purpose and the effects of language

A04 Excellent vocabulary succinctly sums up events

Boxer represents all that is good in Orwell's novella. Our first introduction to him emphasises both his physical power (he has 'vast hairy hoofs' and is as strong 'as any two ordinary horses put together') but also that this 'enormous beast' is a gentle one: he sets his hoofs 'with great care' to avoid hurting any smaller creatures who might be hidden in the straw. Boxer represents, in allegorical form, the purity and virtue of the working man, who in Orwell's eyes is cruelly exploited by both the capitalist system and corrupt political leaders, such as Stalin.

Boxer's strength and physical power is repeatedly mentioned in the story. He is the 'admiration of everybody' on the farm but seems to acquire almost superhuman powers once the revolution is achieved: he seems to be 'more like three horses than one'. The farm is utterly dependent on him: its 'entire work' seems to 'rest upon his mighty shoulders'. Not only does he help to bring in the harvest on time – his 'tremendous muscles' pull the farm through – but his physical strength and dedication are also central to the success of the building (and rebuilding) of the windmill.

Boxer is loyal in every sense. He is also one of the main defenders of the farm from attack. He is a 'terrifying spectacle' rearing up and 'striking out with his great iron-shod hoofs'. Orwell makes clear that Boxer's 'terrifying' power is only ever a force for good: even when fighting for the survival of the farm, Boxer 'sorrowfully' mourns the apparent death of the stable-lad. Orwell is also careful to tell us that this act of violence is not deliberate: 'I forgot that I was wearing iron shoes. Who will believe that I did not do this on purpose?' This contrasts with the calculated terror we see Napoleon dispense during the rest of the story but also shows Orwell's refusal to present Boxer as anything other than saintly. Even in self-defence Boxer's power is benign. And, of course, he turns out not to have killed the stable-lad after all.

A03

Excellent understanding of context in which the book was written and genre

A01

Personal interpretation, which is supported by reference to the text and shows awareness of authorial intention

In fact, Boxer is placed so far beyond reproach that at times Orwell's depiction of his selflessness almost feels exaggerated. Even when he collapses with a damaged lung, Boxer's first thought is for the farm, telling the other animals that he has gathered enough stone for them to rebuild the windmill. Orwell presents him as a paragon of virtue as he is the true hero of the story – the blame-free working man whose trusting, honest nature is exploited by unscrupulous political leaders. While Boxer represents the Stakhanovite workers whose effort and sacrifice was celebrated by the Soviet Union, the book's subtitle ('A Fairy Story') should also be taken into account. Perhaps this is one reason why at times Boxer feels a little one-dimensional – you don't get complex characters in fairy tales, after all.

A04

A range of sentence structure used for clarity and purpose

Boxer has a single weakness. Boxer's lack of intelligence means that he never gets beyond his 'ABCD'. Orwell suggests that physical power is of no use here: Boxer tries 'with all his might' to remember the rest of the alphabet but can never do so. Orwell suggests that this, coupled with his trusting nature, makes him vulnerable to exploitation. When Snowball is expelled from the farm, Boxer is 'vaguely troubled' but cannot articulate his concerns – or, as 'vaguely' suggests, even pinpoint what those concerns are. He tries hard 'to marshall his thoughts' but cannot 'think of anything to say'. He eventually settles for trusting his leader rather than questioning him: 'from then on he adopted the maxim "Napoleon is always right".

A01

A concise, well-expressed summary of the main argument

If 'Animal Farm' has a hero, then it is Boxer. His strength and kindness (traditionally heroic virtues) are vital to the farm's survival but eventually run out. It is no match for the greater, more durable power of the pigs' intelligence or the ruthlessness with which they use it.

VERY HIGH LEVEL

Comment
This is a confident and well-argued response, which shows an excellent understanding of authorial intention and of the book as a whole. This is coupled with a clear, well-supported personal interpretation of the text. Expression is sophisticated and precise. An excellent response.

PRACTICE TASK

Write a full-length response to this exam-style question and then use the **Mark scheme** on page 88 to assess your own response.

> **Question:** How do the sheep and dogs enable Napoleon to seize and maintain power in *Animal Farm*?
>
> Write about:
>
> - What the sheep and dogs do in *Animal Farm* and who they represent
> - How they help Napoleon to control the other farm animals

TOP TIP

You can use the General skills section of the **Mark scheme** on page 88 to remind you of the key criteria you'll need to cover.

Remember:

- Plan quickly and efficiently by using key words from the question.
- Focus on the techniques Orwell uses and the effect of these on the reader.
- Support your ideas with relevant evidence, including quotations.

FURTHER QUESTIONS

 'Rebellion! I do not know when that Rebellion will come, it might be in a week or in a hundred years, but I know, as surely as I see this straw beneath my feet, that sooner or later justice will be done' (Major). Explore the importance of rebellion in *Animal Farm*.

2 'These two disagreed at every point where disagreement was possible. If one of them suggested sowing a bigger acreage with barley, the other was certain to demand a bigger acreage of oats' Explore the relationship between Snowball and Napoleon in *Animal Farm*.

3 Answer both parts of this question:

a) Read the extract in which Napoleon and his dogs threaten and kill other animals on the farm from 'Presently the tumult died down ...' to 'They too were slaughtered ...' (Ch. 7, pp. 52–3).

Compare how the effects of threats and violence are presented in this extract: You should consider:

- the situations faced by the victims of threats and violence and how they react to them
- how the writers' use of language and techniques creates effects.

AND

b) Explore another moment in *Animal Farm* that shows how the pigs control the other animals.

LITERARY TERMS

allegory	a story with two different meanings, where the straightforward meaning on the surface is used to reveal a deeper meaning underneath
anthropomorphic	a description of animals that are seen to behave like humans. They talk and think, for example
beast fable	a fable that makes use of anthropomorphic characters
euphemism	a more pleasant or sanitised way of saying something unpleasant or offensive
euphoria	a feeling of great joy
fable	a short story that contains a moral
genre	a type of literature, for instance poetry, drama, biography, fiction; or style of literature, for example, gothic or romantic
imagery	descriptive language that uses images to make actions, objects and characters more vivid in the reader's mind. Metaphors and similes are examples of Imagery
imperative	verbs used to give orders or instructions
irony	when someone deliberately says one thing when they mean another, usually in a humorous or sarcastic way
jargon	language that has a pretentious vocabulary or meaning, often linked to particular subjects or professions
maxim	a short and effective statement which suggests ideal ways of behaving
metaphor	a form of comparison. One thing is described by saying it *is* another thing, for example: 'All the world's a stage'
narrator (narrative voice)	the voice telling the story or relating a sequence of events (the viewpoint from which a story is told)
novella	a story that is longer than a short story but not quite long enough to be considered a novel
obfuscation	the deliberate use of words to mislead an audience
omniscient narrator	a storyteller with God-like knowledge of the story's world. They can see all the characters' thoughts and actions and can tell the story from several viewpoints
oxymoronic	a phrase or group of words that contradict each other, for example: 'dark light'
pathos	a moment that makes us feel pity or sorrow
propaganda	the deliberate and organised spread of information to make sure that people unquestioningly believe what you want them to believe. It is also used to refer to the information itself. Propaganda is not in itself good or bad – it depends on the purposes to which it is put and on who the audience is and what it believes
protagonist	the main character whose journey we follow in a literary work
proverb (proverbial)	a short saying that deals with a generally accepted truth, for example, 'Too many cooks spoil the broth'
pseudonym	a name that a person uses instead of their real name
register	a style of language, with a particular vocabulary and sentence structure, used for a particular reason or by a group of people
rhetoric	the art of speaking (and writing) effectively so as to persuade an audience
rhetorical question	a question that does not require an answer but is used to emphasise a particular point

satire	literature that targets an issue, institution or idea and attacks it in such a way as to make it look ridiculous or worthy of contempt. It is not the same as simply making fun of something, as the satirical writer has a purpose in attacking the target, other than making people laugh
simile	a way of comparing two things by saying one is *like* the other, for example: 'My love is like a red, red rose'
slogan	a short, memorable phrase, commonly used in advertising, for example: 'Just do it'
stereotype (stereotypical)	a stereotype is a common but vastly simplified (and often distorted and offensive) image of a particular group of people, for example, it is stereotypical to say that all bankers are greedy
symbolism	using an object or person to represent something else
theme	a central idea examined by an author
third person narrative	a story that is told by an unseen narrator who does not use 'I', but uses 'he', 'she' and 'they'
utopia	an imagined perfect place or society. The term is taken from Sir Thomas More's book of the same name (published in 1516), which describes such a society

POLITICAL TERMS

Bolsheviks	the radical wing of the Marxist Russian Social Democratic Party. Founded by Lenin, the Bolsheviks came to power in the 1917 October Revolution and eventually changed their name to the Communist Party of the Soviet Union
capitalist	according to Karl Marx, a capitalist is someone who has money and invests it in a business. This person then makes a profit if the business does well
Cold War	the period from 1949 to 1989, which was marked by a diplomatic and political standoff between the Soviet Union and Western powers
collectivise	a term given to the Stalinist policy of forcing groups of kulaks to unite their farms into one collective farm (or *kolkhoz* in Russian). When the kulaks destroyed their crops and animals in protest, they were brutally punished
democracy (democractic)	a government that is elected by the people or their representatives
dictator	a ruler whose decisions do not need anyone else's agreement. Often, in dictatorships, any form of opposition has been abolished, leaving the ruler with absolute power
indoctrination	brainwashing someone into believing a particular opinion
kulak	a land-owning peasant. After the Russian Revolution, the kulaks did not want their farms to be collectivised. From 1929, Stalin began to exterminate them as a class
Leninism	the political teachings and philosophy of Vladimir Ilyich Ulyanov (known by his nickname 'Lenin'), which was based on Marxism. Lenin believed that workers had to become the ruling class before a socialist state could be achieved
Marxist	a follower of the ideas of Karl Marx (1818–83)
proletariat	the lower or working class, especially those living in industrial societies whose only possession (according to Marx) was the value of their work
republic	a country that elects its leaders and where the head of government is not a monarch
socialism (socialist)	a form of government based on state ownership of a country's assets and services, which also divides its wealth equally among its citizens
spin doctor	a propagandist, usually employed in government, who advises or offers favourable interpretations of policies or events
subversion (subversive)	in political terms, subversion is the act of undermining or attempting to destroy something, particularly a government (often behind the scenes/in secret)
totalitarian	description of a government that has absolute control over its citizens' lives and does not allow them to raise any opposition. Most dictatorships are totalitarian
Tsar	the emperor of Russia until 1914. The word is also used to mean a tyrant or – more generally – a person in authority
tyrant (tyranny)	a person who governs in an unjust and violent way. Tyranny is unjust and violent rule or a state that is governed in this way
undemocratic	see democracy

CHECKPOINT ANSWERS

CHECKPOINT 1, page 9

They provide a framework by which we judge the pigs' later actions.

CHECKPOINT 2, page 10

The animals' names often suit their personalities and draw attention to a particular characteristic. Napoleon was a French emperor who was widely regarded as a tyrant; this is an effective and economical way of getting information across to a reader. For more examples, see **Part Three: Characters**.

CHECKPOINT 3, page 11

The way that Jones mistreats the animals makes us feel sympathetic towards them. Orwell also spends some time introducing the animals. We get to know their characters and start to care about them. Then, when Major tells us how badly mankind treats the animals, we feel sympathetic towards them.

CHECKPOINT 4, page 13

Snowball and Napoleon are introduced as 'Pre-eminent among the pigs' (Ch. 2, p. 9) and so we are alerted to their importance in the book. Look at the individual descriptions that follow this quotation and how they hint about future events.

CHECKPOINT 5, page 14

The fact that the animals remain speechless when they walk through the farmhouse is not seen as sinister in Chapter 2. However, later in the book, the animals' inability to express their thoughts and opinions is one reason why the pigs are able to exploit them further. Look at which animals are able to articulate their feelings and whether or not they do so.

CHECKPOINT 6, page 16

The animals' reading abilities – and their attitudes to education – vary considerably and reinforce certain stereotypes about them. Look at what the different animals choose to read too (Ch. 3, p. 20): for example, the dogs read only the Commandments, showing their fanatical support for the pigs' regime.

CHECKPOINT 7, page 16

The use of the word 'almost' in this quotation suggests that such divisions do already exist on the farm.

CHECKPOINT 8, page 17

Squealer's use of the word 'duty' (Ch. 3, p. 22) suggests that the pigs are responsible for the wellbeing of the other animals on the farm. Squealer presents the pigs' greed as an act of self-sacrifice to the other animals. The pigs' grip on power tightens in this chapter.

CHECKPOINT 9, page 17

The use of the word 'order' (Ch. 3, p. 22) tells us that the pigs are now making decisions without consulting the other animals. The idea of equality on Animal Farm is being abandoned – you do not order your equal to do something, you ask them! Not only are the pigs taking control, but they are also using their power for selfish reasons.

CHECKPOINT 10, page 18

Orwell shows us how unpleasant the humans in *Animal Farm* are so that, even after Napoleon has taken power, we do not think that the solution to the animals' problems is to return to life under Mr Jones or another human. The fact that life on Animal Farm is worse than on the farms run by humans shows just how corrupt and cruel Napoleon has become.

CHECKPOINT 11, page 20

Mollie's love of sugar – as well as her love of ribbons – shows us that she is only interested in her own wellbeing. The sugar is given to her by the humans and shows her willing enslavement to them. Mollie isn't interested in the politics of the farm around her – only in superficial rewards.

CHECKPOINT 12, page 20

Napoleon spends his time between meetings 'canvassing support' (Ch. 5, p. 29) from the other animals and uses the sheep's bleating to silence his opponents. Napoleon, we are told, 'seemed to be biding his time' (Ch. 5, p. 30) and Napoleon's planning is evident when we see the puppies emerging as savage guard dogs.

CHECKPOINT 13, page 21

With clever language, Squealer convinces the animals that Snowball is a criminal and says that Napoleon is protecting them from their own stupidity and the threat of Mr Jones's return. The animals are made to feel guilty for questioning Napoleon and are frightened by the possibility that Mr Jones might come back. The dogs' presence also intimidates them into accepting what they are told.

CHECKPOINT 14, page 23

Squealer asks the animals if they can produce any written evidence of a resolution against trade. The animals, of course, cannot and even if they could, it is doubtful that they would be able to understand it. Squealer uses the animals' ignorance against them.

CHECKPOINT 15, page 24

When the four pigs confess to colluding with Snowball, we are told that 'the dogs promptly tore their throats out' (Ch. 7, p. 52). Eventually there is a 'pile of corpses' and 'the smell of blood' (Ch. 7, p. 53). Orwell describes the executions in a calm and detached way that emphasises their horror.

CHECKPOINT 16, page 25

Napoleon does not deserve his medals, as his cowardly actions at the Battle of the Cowshed show. The fact that he awards them to himself shows that they have no merit and are simply there to make him appear brave and add to his prestige as the leader of Animal Farm.

CHECKPOINT 17, page 28

The pigs' ribbons remind of us of Mollie. She was told by Snowball that ribbons were 'the badge of slavery' (Ch. 2, p. 10). The pigs now wear green ribbons to show that they belong to an elite – ribbons are now a mark of distinction, as well as emphasising the pigs' links to mankind.

CHECKPOINT 18, page 29

There is only one candidate for leadership of Animal Farm: Napoleon. The election is not a free or democratic one. The claim that the farm is a republic is false. The animals have no say in how the farm is run.

CHECKPOINT 19, page 30

The pigs behave like parasites – they do very little work and thrive at the expense of the other animals. They live very comfortably in the farmhouse and eat well while the others starve. Napoleon is being hypocritical.

PROGRESS AND REVISION CHECK ANSWERS

PART TWO, page 32

SECTION ONE: CHECK YOUR KNOWLEDGE

1. The big barn
2. Bluebell, Jessie and Pitcher
3. Rats
4. Beasts of England
5. 'an old spelling book which had belonged to Mr Jones's children' (Ch. 2, p. 14)
6. 'No animal shall kill any other animal' (Ch. 2, p. 15)
7. To tame the rats and rabbits
8. Mollie
9. Squealer
10. Boxer
11. Napoleon
12. Snowball and Mr Frederick
13. Snowball
14. Squealer
15. Because he is drunk
16. Selling Boxer to the knacker
17. A corner of the pasture
18. Benjamin and Clover
19. Napoleon
20. The ace of spades

SECTION TWO: CHECK YOUR UNDERSTANDING

Task 1

- What we are told about Snowball in Chapter 2: 'quicker in speech and more inventive' (Ch. 2, p. 9).
- Innovator and educator – the Committees, reading classes, plans for the windmill.
- Not necessarily better than Napoleon: takes part in the seizure of the milk and apples and is unrepentant when it seems that the stable-lad had been killed.

- Becomes a scapegoat for the farm's misfortunes after he has fled, an 'invisible' (Ch. 7, p. 49) presence who is said to be in league with the farm's enemies.

Task 2

- Four pigs protest at the meeting, showing that not every pig agrees with Napoleon's actions.
- They protest as the Sunday meetings were meant to be an opportunity for the animals to debate the farm's decisions (although the animals can 'never think of any resolutions of their own' (Ch.3, p. 19)). Napoleon sees these democratic debates as a waste of time, and by cancelling the meetings, moves the farm towards dictatorship.
- The pigs are silenced by the dogs' growling and the sheep's bleating drowns out any possibility of further protest.
- They are forced to confess to obviously fabricated crimes in Chapter 7 and are slaughtered.
- This mirrors the way that opposition is silenced elsewhere in the story (e.g. Boxer is marked out by Squealer) and shows the techniques Napoleon (and Stalin) used to keep power.

PART THREE, page 50

SECTION ONE: CHECK YOUR KNOWLEDGE

1. Mr Frederick
2. Squealer
3. Muriel
4. Clover
5. Snowball
6. Snowball
7. Benjamin
8. Minimus
9. Mr Pilkington
10. Moses

SECTION TWO: CHECK YOUR UNDERSTANDING

- Orwell presents Boxer as one of the most sympathetic characters in the story: see his regret at hurting the stable-lad.
- He carries 'the entire work of the farm … upon his massive shoulders' (Ch. 3, p. 17) and is central to the farm's survival after the revolution: harvest, Battles of the Cowshed and Windmill.
- Major predicts his fate – but we don't imagine it will happen under the pigs.
- Once the hero of the story has been killed, the farm rapidly descends into greater tyranny.

PART FOUR, page 60

SECTION ONE: CHECK YOUR KNOWLEDGE

1. Joseph Stalin's
2. Trotsky's victorious leadership of the Red Army to defeat invading forces during the Russian Civil War
3. Trotsky and Stalin
4. Orwell believed that political language was used to manipulate the truth and make outrageous ideas sound acceptable.
5. Orwell was a lifelong socialist.
6. The Spanish Civil War
7. The BBC Eastern Service
8. Marx believed that in a capitalist society workers were exploited by the people (capitalists) they worked for.
9. The Battle of Stalingrad, part of the German invasion of Soviet Russia
10. 'Anthropomorphic' means the description of animals as though they are human.

SECTION TWO: CHECK YOUR UNDERSTANDING

- Immediately after the revolution, he rewards the animals with food.
- He works in secret to build a power base: canvassing support for his schemes and taking the puppies away and hiding them.
- He uses the dogs and sheep to suppress opposition and terrify the animals into agreeing with him.
- He uses Squealer to control what information the animals have and to make them doubt their own memories and ideas.

PART FIVE, page 67

SECTION ONE: CHECK YOUR KNOWLEDGE

1. 'A Fairy Story'
2. An omniscient, third person narrator
3. Writing that targets an issue or idea and attacks it in such a way as to make it look ridiculous
4. Because they *are* working as slaves – for Napoleon
5. He shows Napoleon carrying a whip, which was seen as an instrument of torture under Jones.
6. A short story that contains a moral, usually with animals as characters
7. A very simplified (and often distorted and offensive) image of a group of people
8. The Seven Commandments
9. The windmill represents Stalin's industrialisation of Russia and the sacrifices made by the Russian people under his Five-Year Plans.
10. A form of language, often linked to a particular group of people or profession, that has a pretentious or confusing vocabulary

SECTION TWO: CHECK YOUR UNDERSTANDING

- We expect to find anthropomorphic characters in a fairy story and an omniscient narrator.
- We expect a straightforward plot with a clear ending.
- We expect to see good triumph over evil – this doesn't happen in *Animal Farm* (neither is there a clear ending).
- By playing with our expectations, Orwell subverts the genre and uses it for satiric effect. *Animal Farm* is no fairy story.

MARK SCHEME

POINTS YOU COULD HAVE MADE

- The sheep are seen as unintelligent. Snowball has to simplify Animalism into a slogan so that they can understand it.
- Orwell uses the sheep allegorically to represent the damage that mob rule can do and how it can be manipulated to silence free speech.
- They are only ever described as a group – no individual stands out.
- Orwell uses the sheep to suggest that the simplification of language ('Four legs good, two legs bad', Ch. 3, p. 21) can restrict thought.

- The dogs are seen as savage from the start, when they chase the rats during Major's speech in Chapter 1.
- The puppies are removed by Napoleon in secret and without the farm's agreement.
- The dogs help Napoleon to control the animals through fear. The executions terrify them and their 'menacing' (Ch. 5, p. 34) presence means Squealer never encounters real opposition.
- They show us that Napoleon has become as evil as Jones – they 'wagged their tails' (Ch. 5, p. 34) in the same way towards him.

GENERAL SKILLS

Make a judgement about your level based on the points you made (above) and the skills you showed.

Level	Key elements	Spelling, punctuation and grammar	Tick your level
Very high	**Very well-structured answer which gives a rounded and convincing viewpoint.** You use very detailed analysis of the writer's methods and effects on the reader, using precise references which are fluently woven into what you say. You draw inferences, consider more than one perspective or angle, including the context where relevant, and make interpretations about the text as a whole.	You spell and punctuate with consistent accuracy, and use a very wide range of vocabulary and sentence structures to achieve effective control of meaning.	
Good to High	**A thoughtful, detailed response with well-chosen references.** At the top end, you address all aspects of the task in a clearly expressed way, and examine key aspects in detail. You are beginning to consider implications, explore alternative interpretations or ideas; at the top end, you do this fairly regularly and with some confidence.	You spell and punctuate with considerable accuracy, and use a considerable range of vocabulary and sentence structures to achieve general control of meaning.	
Mid	**A consistent response with clear understanding of the main ideas shown.** You use a range of references to support your ideas and your viewpoint is logical and easy to follow. Some evidence of commenting on writers' effects, though more needed.	You spell and punctuate with reasonable accuracy, and use a reasonable range of vocabulary and sentence structures.	
Lower	**Some relevant ideas but an inconsistent and rather simple response in places.** You show you have understood the task and you make some points to support what you say, but the evidence is not always well chosen. Your analysis is a bit basic and you do not comment in much detail on the writer's methods.	Your spelling and punctuation is inconsistent and your vocabulary and sentence structures are both limited. Some of these make your meaning unclear.	